"In *Inspired Leadership*, Gaskell passes along fantastic insights from his personal experience of leading some of the world's great brands, building new companies and revitalising stalled businesses. His knowledge—often gained the hard way—helps leaders appreciate that building an extraordinary team with ordinary people is simple, but not easy. Inspired leaders recognise their own strengths and weaknesses, provide continuous coaching and pay attention to their team. Inspiring leaders encourage teams to share beliefs and strive for common goals and in doing so they create something special and successful and fun. Read this book and use the process to build your own success".

Marshall Goldsmith, World's #1 Leadership Thinker

"In any performance situation leadership is what makes the greatest difference. Not only from the person designated as leader but when displayed by everyone in the team. Inspired Leaders are those special leaders able to ensure that every team member is engaged and able to fully contribute their ideas and energy. *Inspired Leadership* offers any leader, at any level, an indispensable guide to ensuring their team perform at the top of their game every day".

Sir Clive Woodward OBE,
England Rugby World Cup Winning Coach, Team GB Director

"The lessons in this book are applicable to any commercial sector, or indeed any team. Working with Kevin we have applied his structured approach to the music and entertainment industry. We have taken his advice, tools and process and created a hugely successful business of inspired musicians performing extraordinary music for audiences all over the world".

Chris White, Dire Straits, The Dire Straits Experience

"Teamwork is critical to success at the highest level. Team members need leaders who see beyond the obvious and generate ideas with wider reaching impact. Being part of implementing those ideas is exciting. This is possible when Inspired Leadership is demonstrated at all levels in the team. This book shows how to achieve this level of inspiration and success in the real world".

Lewis Moody MBE, England Captain, British and Irish Lions

INSPIRED LEADERSHIP

INSPIRED LEADERSHIP

HOW YOU CAN ACHIEVE
EXTRAORDINARY RESULTS IN BUSINESS

KEVIN GASKELL

WILEY

This edition first published 2017
© 2017 Kevin Gaskell

Registered office
John Wiley & Sons Ltd, The Atrium, Southern Gate, Chichester, West Sussex, PO19 8SQ, United Kingdom

For details of our global editorial offices, for customer services and for information about how to apply for permission to reuse the copyright material in this book please see our website at www.wiley.com.

Library of Congress Cataloging-in-Publication Data is available

A catalogue record for this book is available from the British Library.

ISBN 978-1-119-38302-4 (pbk) ISBN 978-1-119-38313-0 (ebk)
ISBN 978-1-119-38310-9 (ebk)

Cover design: Wiley

Set in 10/14.5pt ITCFranklinGothicStd-Book by Thomson Digital, Noida, India
Printed in Great Britain by TJ International Ltd, Padstow, Cornwall, UK

10 9 8 7 6 5 4 3 2

CONTENTS

ACKNOWLEDGEMENTS

This book is written with grateful thanks to everyone with whom I have shared my business journey and adventures. The stories told and the many lessons learnt have their roots in the times when we committed and won – and occasionally when we battled but lost.

Along the way I have met inspiring people, too many to name, who have taught me all that I know about leadership and success. Those people lived their own journey and I am grateful that the crossing of our paths meant that we could share some adventures and wins.

My journey could not have been possible without the enduring patience of my family and friends who never ceased to support me while I immersed myself in the companies I led. Each of you have inspired me and kept me grounded in the real world and for that I am eternally thankful.

This book was in the planning phase for some time but it would not have happened without the expert support of Tim Phillips. He turned my memories, principles and philosophy into a readable structure.

I have written this book with the primary intention of encouraging the inspiring leaders of the future. Whether you are a new leader setting out on your leadership journey, or an experienced leader facing a challenge which is offering you an opportunity to learn and grow, I hope that you will find inspiration and techniques in these pages. Use this book to support you, challenge you and allow you to reach your own vision of success.

Never forget, most limitations are self-imposed, so remove them and fly.

Kevin Gaskell
April 2017

ABOUT THE AUTHOR

 Kevin Gaskell is widely considered to be one of the outstanding leaders of his generation. The youngest ever Managing Director of Porsche, Lamborghini and BMW, he led all three companies to record growth and performance. He then walked away to follow his own passion and learn the hard way what it takes to found and build a great company from just a good idea.

He has enjoyed 25 years of success as a business leader, founding startups, driving turnarounds and leading major brands in sectors from technology to gardening. The teams he has led have created over £3 billion in shareholder value.

In this book, he shares his experiences of repeatedly inspiring teams to achieve extraordinary performance in businesses ranging from 7 to 7,000 employees. Using practical examples from his own companies he shows how the real difference between good and great performance is made by the people whom he calls inspired leaders.

Inspired leaders are catalysers for positive change. They bring an infectious energy, high expectation, excitement and an intense motivation. This book shares the methods, tools and practical techniques used by inspired leaders and invites the reader to become such a leader able to build teams, build businesses and achieve extraordinary results in the real world.

Kevin is a serial entrepreneur and investor. His portfolio of companies has received awards including: best private equity investment performance of the year, strategic ecommerce business of the year, world's seventh most innovative company and Insight Innovation winner Europe.

He is active as a turnaround expert and strategist and is a frequent international conference speaker on the topics of inspired leadership, the future customer and the impact of digital technology.

He can be contacted at www.kevingaskell.com or through his company 'The Inspired Leaders Group' at www.theinspiredleaders.com.

INTRODUCTION

Ordinary people can do extraordinary things

Impossible is just a big word thrown around by small men who find it easier to live the world they've been given than to explore the power they have to change it.

Muhammad Ali

When I speak to groups in companies or at conferences about the work I have done, I tell the audience that ordinary people, led well, can achieve extraordinary things. I know this is true, because I have seen it happen, over and over again, throughout my career. I have been privileged to see teams that I have led do things and achieve business results that, at the beginning, no one believed were possible.

Afterwards, when the audience asks questions, one of the most frequent is: "what should I do to motivate people?" I used to get confused by the question, because often they wanted to know about prizes, incentives and bonuses, and that wasn't what I was talking about. Then I realized: they could ask a question that sounds similar, but is entirely different. What should I do to inspire people?

The answer to this question is what this book is about, because that's what I have tried to do, every day, for the last 25 years. I can't tell you how to motivate other people, because that's their internal emotion. What I hope you will do is to learn to inspire them to find their own motivation. They will do extraordinary things that transform their work and their lives, things they didn't think were possible. They will feel the thrill of success, creativity and the satisfaction of trust and integrity. In turn, they will hopefully inspire the people around them, and the next generation of leaders that will follow. That's how great businesses are built.

You can do all this.

You cannot, however, do it if you do not give them a dream to commit to, if you fail to explain to them what you are going to do and listen to their ideas, or if you fail to build a culture that will encourage and support them to fly. Weak leaders lie, bully and rely on financial incentives. They hide the truth and look for scapegoats. They overvalue themselves and undervalue team members based on status, rather than contribution. And then they look for ways to "motivate" their unhappy teams to do jobs that they find meaningless. Unfortunately, many of these leaders are then sent, or even promoted, to poison another group.

Every success that I have been involved with happened because the people who created it, whether they were cleaners, managers or owners, were inspired to find their own motivation. It comes from inside, it encourages you to be the best you can be, and it will help you take responsibility for your own goals. When your teams find it and start to create their own magic, it can be the best feeling in the world.

For 25 years I have been helping to inspire the people around me to do things they never thought possible. Along the way they have achieved results that exceeded my ambitions for them. They have amazed themselves at what became possible. They have transformed their jobs, their lives and the lives of their families.

If you know how to inspire those around you, they stop trying to chase immediate rewards, and they start thinking about building something that lasts, making meaningful changes to the lives of their customers, their colleagues and themselves. They want to achieve deeper, more satisfying goals. Motivation lasts as long as the incentive does. Inspiration lasts a lifetime, and beyond.

You can be a leader

This book is my way to pass on what I have learned – often the hard way – and help you to do the same for other people. I made plenty of mistakes along the way, and I will tell you about some of them, too, because I learned as much from the low points – and there have been terrible lows – as from the highs. Also, I have worked and travelled with some remarkable leaders who have helped me to achieve things that I did not think were possible. This book has many lessons that I learned from them too.

I hope that you are reading this book because you want to be an inspirational leader. The team you lead may be large, spread over many countries, or it may be small and local – it doesn't matter. I have learnt that there's no team or task too small or too big to think about in this way.

I learned leadership on the job, as you will have to. But the methods I used are, mostly, the same things I have applied throughout my career to turnarounds, startups and adventures. I'll describe a number of real situations and examples in this book, when I believe they help to understand how I think about leadership, and what has worked for me.

How will we do this? The book is based on methods that I have applied over and over again, in large blue-chip brand names like Porsche and BMW, but also helping extraordinary small startup businesses realize their dreams. When my son and I walked together to the North and South Poles to help fund the construction of a leukaemia treatment unit, we used these ideas.

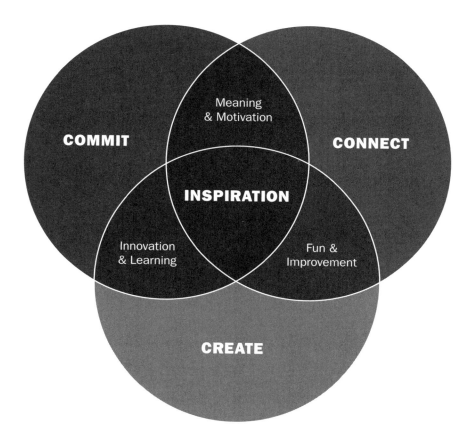

There are three parts of the process, and three parts to the book. If you want to be an inspiring leader, I am going to ask you to Commit, to Connect and to Create.

Commit

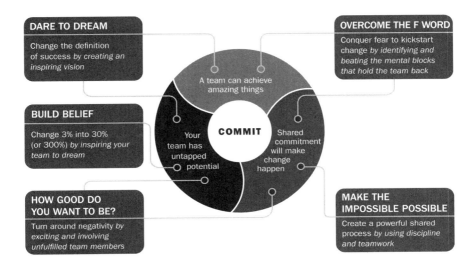

Every successful businessperson is a dreamer. So the first step to your team achieving extraordinary things is when together you commit to making that dream real. You cannot be an inspiring leader unless you commit absolutely, and can share that commitment. You are not saying you'll do the job, you are making a decision to achieve a goal. When you make the decision, you do it absolutely, with determination, with passion and with conviction.

We've all made a vague, spontaneous commitment in a conversation, a meeting or in a bar. Maybe we believed it for a moment, but by the time the words are out of our mouths we know, deep inside, that we don't seriously intend to keep to it. The commitment I'm talking about here is not a spontaneous thing. It comes with integrity. It is what you are.

You dare to dream You change the definition of success by creating an inspiring vision of what it could look like.

You build belief You can change ambition to grow by 3% into a vision of 30% or 300% by inspiring your team with your vision. You issue an

invitation to the team to forget the numbers and to share an exciting
journey to success.

You challenge: how good do you want to be? No matter what the situation is, you switch on positive feelings by exciting unfulfilled team members with the possibilities of what the team can achieve.

You make the impossible possible You create a powerful shared process by using discipline and teamwork. Most limitations are self-imposed, so take them away.

You confront the F word You conquer fear to kickstart change by identifying and beating the mental blocks that hold back the team.

Connect

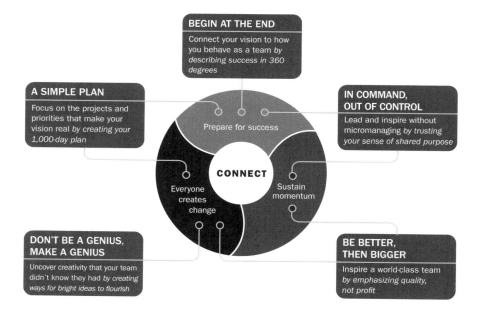

Connecting is about helping everybody in the business discover and value their role in creating change. They might not be used to thinking that they can do this, or even that any change at all is a good idea. But we know, and I have experienced, the difference that this connection can make to a team. Not least because it makes it possible for you to plan and to share ownership of the plan with the team.

You begin at the end You connect your vision to how you behave as a team by describing success in 360 degrees.

You make a simple plan You focus on the projects and priorities that will make your vision real and instil urgency by creating a 1,000-day plan.

You don't need to be a genius because you make a genius You uncover creativity that your team didn't know they had by creating ways for bright ideas to flourish.

You become better first, then bigger You inspire a world-class team by emphasizing quality, not profit.

You are in command, and out of control You lead and inspire without micromanaging by trusting your sense of shared purpose.

Create

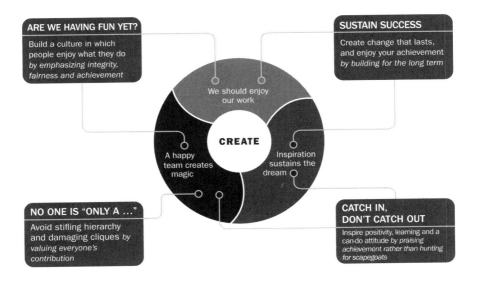

Teams create magic when they are challenged, united and happy in their work, whatever the scale of the task. To do this, you have to build a culture of continuous change and innovation, at every level, and sustain it.

You have fun You build a culture in which people enjoy what they do by emphasizing integrity, fairness and achievement.

You understand that no one is an "only a ..." You avoid stifling hierarchy and damaging cliques by valuing everyone's contribution.

You catch in, and don't catch out You inspire positivity, learning and can-do attitude by praising achievement rather than hunting for scapegoats.

You sustain success You create change that lasts, and enjoy your achievement by building for the long term.

Leadership is about learning

If you want to lead, you will make mistakes. This is normal, we have all done it. What matters is that you listen to those around you, and learn from them – even if you hear things that you might not like. None of this works without a principle that I call OVT: One Version of the Truth.

OVT does not mean, however, that your opinion as leader must be that version of the truth.

I have tried to be as honest as possible in this book, about mistakes as well as successes. But everyone sees the world through their eyes, and sometimes we forget the bad times. So, in writing this book, I called up some of my colleagues from the past. I asked them what they remembered about the work we did together. Was it how I remembered it? There was one condition: be honest. Some of what they told me is quoted in the book, but their influence runs through every page of it.

I have also gone back into my notebooks. I have kept a notebook of my work for every leadership job I have attempted. When I wrote them I tried to be honest, and capture my feelings, fears and ideas. Looking back at them now, I can remember the moments, and how it felt. They are not just a record, they are something I learned from, and a reminder every day of both the good and the bad parts. I'd recommend that you do the same, but with the same rule for yourself that you use with others: be honest.

Using your honesty and these principles, you can inspire yourself, and the people around you, to achieve extraordinary things together. When you inspire your team with your leadership, ordinary people can do extraordinary things. I've seen it happen, and this book will show you how.

Part One

Commit

Chapter 1

Dare to Dream

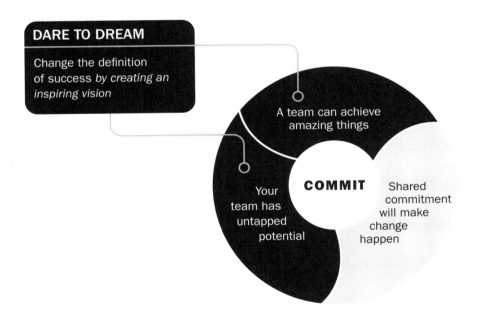

DARE TO DREAM

Change the definition of success *by creating an inspiring vision*

A team can achieve amazing things

Your team has untapped potential

COMMIT

Shared commitment will make change happen

E very inspiring leader is a dreamer first.

When I try to convince a leadership team that they can achieve something that's extraordinary, I always say to them, "Never start with the numbers. Start by imagining what this business could be." As an inspiring leader your first goal is to change the definition of success, and commit to a bigger, better dream. This may scare you at first. But we will make that leap. It may take you a while to see the power behind the commitment to dream but, if you can't commit, then the rest of this book will have little meaning for you.

This chapter will introduce the fundamental principle of inspiring leadership. At the end of it, you will be ready to use dreams to inspire your team.

Over the years I have found that this works for teams, and businesses, that are large and small. People often say to me: "It's all very well for you, because you make all the decisions for the company. That's easy. I just run a little department."

And I say, "It makes no difference. Do it for yourself. Nobody is going to tell you you're wrong when your team and your results start to improve."

Being a leader

If you're going to lead this change, we need to agree on what a leader is.

Warren Bennis invented the study of leadership in companies in the 1950s, and he had strong views on what leaders are, and are not. Having grown up in the Great Depression and served in the Second World War, he used his experiences, and what he learned in his research, to advise countless CEOs and at least three US presidents.

He believed that leadership is about using the power to achieve change, and that good leaders were marked out by humanity and humility as well as business results. "A leader is someone whose actions have the most profound consequences on other people's lives, for better or for worse, sometimes for ever and ever," he wrote.

Bennis also thought that too much of what we call leadership is nothing of the sort. It is management, which is important, but management is all about implementing what other people believe to be correct. All businesses need managers, but all teams also need leaders, and they are rarer. Bennis made this distinction in his research. He used to tell people that a leader both does things right, but also *does the right thing*. That managers help you get where you want to go, but leaders can tell you *what it is you want*. And that managers keep their attention on the bottom line, but that leaders *are looking at the horizon.*

So what sort of people are these leaders? I argue that everyone, in some situation, can learn to be a leader. In the past, many people thought that leaders were born that way, and tried to make a list of the personality traits of historical leaders like Winston Churchill, Nelson Mandela or Steve Jobs to examine what they had in common.

The result: not much. This type of research usually produces a list of traits like self-confidence, assertiveness and a need for achievement. The problem comes when we try to apply that to other people: while leaders might have these traits, there are many more people who have a need for achievement who are terrible leaders. This is good news for us, because it suggests that inspiring leaders aren't created at birth. You can learn to be an inspiring leader.

Other research has asked how leaders behave – rather than looking at the common principles of leaders, they look for what's common about leadership. This helps me to understand my observations. I have found that good leaders don't get blown off course by today's events, or even worry too much about them. And I have learnt, like many people before me, that failure is inevitable, and what matters is being flexible enough to change your mind when things go wrong.

But, of course, different situations require different types of behaviour. Leadership behaviour in a situation where safety is critical is not the same as it is in an informal team. You can't run a startup like an army regiment, or vice versa. So when researchers in the 1960s tried to make similar lists of how leaders behaved, they found that the list was too long to be useful.

So, perhaps, are the best leaders the ones who know how to change according to the situation? The point of being a leader is that you will be able to make a difference, and so you can choose, at least to some extent, how to do that. This "situational model" was developed by Kenneth Blanchard and Paul Hersey, and they identified four distinct leadership styles: Telling, Selling, Participating and Delegating, depending on the context.

But this still tends to focus on how leaders communicate with the managers who report to them. An inspiring leader has to look at the biggest picture: everyone you are responsible for, the whole team, the whole organization can be transformed if they can find inspiration in the way you lead them. The attributes, behaviour and situational awareness of leaders are useful tools. We are all interested in something bigger.

Inspiring leadership transforms teams, and it transforms lives because you show the people you lead what can be possible, and then, together, you achieve it.

Learning to lead

You can learn to lead at any time. I was lucky, I had the chance to learn early, although it didn't seem lucky at the time. I joined Porsche in the UK in 1987, when I was 27. At the end of the 1980s Porsche's image was associated with the "yuppie" business culture at that time. For good and bad reasons, the brand had become a powerful status symbol. In the film *Crazy People*, an advertising executive played by Dudley Moore decides to tell the truth in his advertising. His (unfair) pitch for Porsche: "It's a little too small to get laid in. But you get laid the minute you get out." It was not a fair reflection of the Porsche brand but it stuck in the public's imagination.

I'd always loved messing about with car engines, and joining the company that was associated with excellence in engineering should have been my dream job, but by the early 1990s, Porsche in the UK was heading for a nasty crash. As with many failing businesses, respect, pride and support had gone out of the window. We didn't have a strategy, any consistency or any vision. We were well on the way to losing 90% of our sales in the UK, but we just kept building cars because nobody made a decision.

This wasn't a secret, because Porsche's sales in all its export markets were hit by the global recession that began on Black Monday, in October 1987. In January 1989, Porsche announced a 52% fall in profits, as US sales had halved the previous year. Group turnover fell by 27%. "The last business year was one of the hardest in the history of Porsche," Walter

Gnauert, the finance director, had told the press. In the UK, we had three years of inventory, literally parked in a number of warehouses and then in a field as they overflowed. Apparently desirable cars that no one wanted to buy. *The Sun* newspaper printed a picture of them on its front page. Porsche was the symbol of the impending recession.

The downturn hit the UK later, in the early 1990s. One of the problems for Porsche was that many of the car owners were entrepreneurs and small businesspeople (the yuppie image of the time was never strictly true). When they had problems with their business in the recession, the entrepreneurs liquidated the easiest assets to get rid of, and so the UK's used car dealerships were flooded with second-hand Porsches.

Adrian Hallmark was sales and marketing manager while I was at Porsche. We were about the same age, and thought about things the same way, and we were equally shocked at what was going on in the business. Adrian went and checked all the orders that we were getting from dealers. He found, to his horror, that they weren't real sales: dealers would pre-order cars so that they were at the front of the queue when a sale did happen. When sales dropped, we were left with the stock.

> "Finding this out was one of the most horrendous business experiences I've had," he recalls, "It took 18 months to clear our stock. It wasn't helped by having newspapers' helicopters flying overhead to take photos of all the cars we hadn't sold. . . . When we unearthed all our problems, we went into corporate denial. We ended up with so much stock because we were too frightened to tell the factory the bad news."

If you have ever been in a failing business, you know that there's a moment when, collectively, no one seems to know what to do, and the company looks for someone to grab it by the scruff of the neck. As is also common, we didn't have anyone who was willing to do it. I was just a young operations manager, but the managing director used to pull me into board meetings in front of the whole Porsche family. He would say, "Welcome! Kevin's going to tell you what's going on." Four years after I had started work at Porsche it felt as if I had taken on more and more responsibility almost by default because nobody else wanted it.

During my teenage years, when British industry was associated with failure, I had been a small part of a successful business which effectively managed itself because the people who worked there, top to bottom, felt that that it was the right thing to do. Fifteen years later, I was part of a business that was associated with extreme success, but which was headed for disaster.

Eventually, at the end of March 1992, the UK Managing Director was relieved of his duties and Porsche's German management showed up at our offices en masse. They sat in the boardroom and they demanded to see me and the German finance manager who had been parachuted in to keep the business afloat. Together, we'd been running around behind the scenes trying to steady the ship. I phoned my wife and I said, "I'm going to get fired today."

I was scared stiff. I was 32, mortgaged over my head, with two young kids.

So we were called into the meeting, and they started to give us a hard time. We had nothing to lose. So, assuming I'd be fired anyway, I said to them: "Hang on. You should be embarrassed. This was entirely predictable. You could see it coming, we could see it coming."

I actually said, "You could fix this."

They said, "What do you mean?"

For four hours, we stood at two flip-charts in front of this German board and explained to them what we would do.

And then they told us to leave the room.

After the meeting was over I phoned my wife and said, "I'm not coming home."

"What happened?" she asked.

I said: "They just made me the managing director."

I had a degree in engineering, a few years of experience as a management accountant, and the idea in my head that, if we could recapture the respect, pride and mutual support that I'd seen in my first job, and if I remembered what my dad had achieved, then maybe we could salvage something.

I started to use these ideas in my first week as managing director of Porsche. I had never run a company before, but I knew we were operating day to day without a clear strategy and we were still spending money we didn't have. In the head office, we employed 260 people, even though our dealers were selling fewer than 2,000 cars a year, and Porsche did all its manufacturing in Germany. In the head office we had our own press office with four staff, an in-house marketing agency, a personnel department. We employed 14 people to develop software, and 12 to do sales planning. On 28 April 1992, I reduced our headcount to 120. We went from 13 departments to 5. It was a dramatic change. Many people told me it was too much change in one go. But the business was failing, so something had to be done to stop the losses, and quickly.

I had been in the company for four years. I knew every employee. I also knew the wives, husbands, kids and even the dogs of the people we let go. It was awful. I went back into my swanky new office, and I locked the door, and I cried my eyes out. This was a defining moment in my journey. The point when I swore I would never again allow a business to get in so much trouble that I had to make mass redundancies, and I never have since.

But, in 1,000 days, we went from losing 20% on each sale to making 20% on each sale. We went from being effectively bust to being the most profitable car company in the country. We went from having three years of inventory to having one year of forward orders. The teams' work drove the company from position 32 (out of 32) to first position, for two consecutive years, in the UK national dealer satisfaction survey.

Adrian remembers the struggle, but like me he remembers an incredibly tough period with affection:

"It wasn't a nightmare, it was quite the opposite. Even though we had lost so many people, the remaining team was utterly engaged, completely committed and they would fight like dogs to make sure the business would come back. We had one mission, we had to make it work. So it is still one of the most enjoyable times I've ever had at work."

The lesson this experience taught me was that dreams can come true – but first of all, you have to know what that dream is.

Abandon 3% thinking

Apple's famous "Think different" advertisement claimed: "The people who are crazy enough to think they can change the world are the only ones who do." When Rob Siltanen, the young copywriter who thought up the line, presented it to Steve Jobs, he hated it. But, when he thought longer about it, Jobs realized it was "a brilliant idea".[1]

It's not just a brilliant idea, it's an inspiring way to live and work. It's not just about making new things, it's about finding entirely new ways to think about what you do, or the service you deliver.

When I meet teams for the first time and ask them where the business is heading they often start the conversation by telling me something like "We want another 3% market share."

I say: "I have no interest in that."

And they say: "Why not?"

"Let's get better first, and bigger will come," I tell them. When you focus on getting better at what you do, you will win your 3%, the next 3%, and the 3% after that, because you're building improvement that is sustainable. You can do this only by thinking differently. The alternative is that you chase a number. You might get there once, but just by picking this number and aiming for it, you have compromised your dream. Let's rebuild what we do, I tell them, and that commitment is far more effective than chasing 3%.

For example, Paul Polman took over as CEO of Unilever in 2009, and a year later created the company's "sustainable living plan". His idea was that Unilever could make the planet a better place. It is halving its environmental impact, will soon draw all of its energy from renewable sources, and is introducing products that help a billion people in poverty live healthy lives. He decided the business was too focused on short-term performance, so he stopped issuing quarterly reports.

Salman Khan, the founder of Khan Academy, used to make YouTube videos to help tutor his cousins. When he noticed that thousands of other kids were watching them, he quit his job at a hedge fund to found his company, saying: "We have a mission for a free, world-class education for anyone, anywhere." Today, Khan Academy provides free tutorials to more than 40 million kids around the world, and has been called "the future of education" by Bill Gates, who is one of his financial backers.

You want to build teams that do extraordinary things. That doesn't happen by accident, so the team need to be committed to the goal. As the leader, their commitment begins as your commitment. And for you to be committed, you have to be truly committed to something bigger than yourself, and something that is worthy of your commitment.

Daring to dream has five elements:

Dreaming breaks rules When you dream, you throw off the constraints that you, and others around you, have lived with. No successful dream is small. You embrace a creative future, and the future is unknown. Most limitations are self-imposed. Choose to take them away.

Dreaming is big Many people around you will encourage you not to rock the boat. Too much of our time is spent creating small plans, with meaningless goals. It doesn't matter if they succeed or fail, because they change little. *Your* dreams will have consequences.

Dreams give us purpose When we dream of a different future, science tells us that we are more likely to achieve our goals.

Dreams inspire change Not all dreams are good, and not all dreamers are leaders. Your success as a leader depends on your ability to take a dream and make it work.

Dreams give you passion If indecision stops you from doing great work, they will help you to make decisions.

Unfortunately, in many businesses the first reaction to difficult times or challenges is to cut costs and lay off staff, instead of saying, "How do we use our resources better? What could we do that's different?" Controlling cost is important (remember, my first major task as a manager was firing half of Porsche's workforce), but it can only ever help your business to survive for the short term. In my experience, it will never change the organization's effectiveness, or allow it to transform and grow to become world class.

Your learning starts now

Why do we need to "dare" to dream? Because the moment you take that first step, as you open your mind to what's possible, you realize that you're stepping into the unknown. It doesn't matter if you are the CEO or the receptionist, daring to dream is risky.

You may have experience, qualifications, competence and an imagination. But you are about to create something new, and you don't know how it will finish, or what will happen next. If I join a new department or company, even as CEO or Chairman, I begin as a learner. That's what I was at Porsche and have been in many businesses since. Knowing next to nothing can be an advantage, because you are looking at your job with a fresh pair of eyes. It helps you ask why. Others around you will tell you that their experience tells them your dream isn't possible. Remember: it is possible to know too much.

At Porsche, we had no choice but to start again. The business was on life support, and our dream wasn't complicated. The next stage of my adventure would be different: could I apply the same approach to a business with thousands of employees and revenues of £3 billion a year, which almost no one believed needed to change?

Note

1. Isaacson, W. 2011. *Steve Jobs*. New York: Simon & Schuster.

Chapter 2

Build Belief

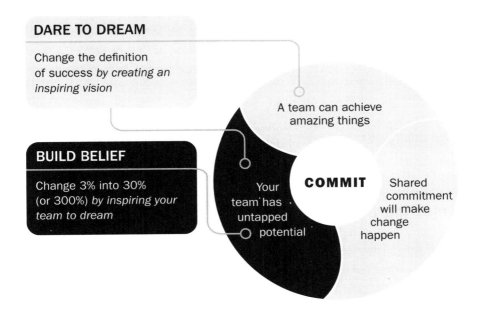

DARE TO DREAM

Change the definition of success *by creating an inspiring vision*

BUILD BELIEF

Change 3% into 30% (or 300%) *by inspiring your team to dream*

A team can achieve amazing things

Your team has untapped potential

COMMIT

Shared commitment will make change happen

Your dream is only as good as the people who believe in it. If you want to create change, then you cannot do it alone, or against the will of the people who work with you. But creating shared belief is never straightforward, especially if some of the team members you are asking to change like the status quo.

In this chapter, we will look at what happened in the job I did immediately after Porsche, when I moved to the position of CEO of BMW GB, and discovered that success can be as big an impediment to culture change as failure.

Finding a sense of shared purpose in a business that previously had treated strategy as a sort of optional extra helped to create growth that was far in excess of what anyone expected.

Rejecting the status quo

In 1994, the British car manufacturer Rover Group plc was acquired by BMW, the German luxury car manufacturer, in a negotiation that took only 10 days. BMW paid £800 million for a manufacturer that it hoped would create economies of scale, as it became involved in mass manufacturing. BMW considered that, until it sold 1 million cars a year, it could be vulnerable in the future. I had always admired BMW's engineering and business, and I thought of Tom Purves, who had risen from an apprenticeship at Rolls Royce to run BMW's business in the UK, as a mentor.

Tom was an experienced, skilled leader who had overseen BMW GB's steady growth. He had been assigned to Rover to represent BMW's interests, and one day in 1996 he visited my office at Porsche for lunch.

"One of my responsibilities is to find my successor," he said, "I think you'd be very good at it."

A few weeks later, I was visiting BMW's high-rise headquarters in Munich. I did six interviews in a day, and every time I got in the lift it went up, so I thought, "As long as this keeps going up I'm doing all right." Eventually the lift went all the way to the top: the last interview of the day was in the office of Bernd Pischetsrieder, BMW's chairman. His office was a curved room and so large that, at first, I only realized he was there from the clouds of cigar smoke that snaked round the corner.

We shook hands. "Welcome to BMW," he said.

At that point, no one had yet asked me what I intended to do. Looking back, they assumed that I would do what they wanted me to do. After all, when you join, you know nothing. But, if you dream, you can't stop yourself from breaking the rules.

When I started, one of BMW's global executives gave me a piece of paper. He said, "That's the plan." In other words, "Just do that, and you will be OK."

BMW was selling 45,000 cars a year in the UK, and the plan – apparently this had become my plan – over the next five years would be to work towards a sales target of 54,000 cars a year. I had been given the job of growing at 3.7% a year. This was not a dream.

I said: "It's not very exciting."

He said: "Kevin, we love what you did at Porsche. But this is a very successful business. Do not knock it off the rails."

Another way to describe his advice: you're in the big leagues now, so do not rock the boat by dreaming. It is a tempting argument, because suddenly many more people rely on you. You, and they, have a long way to fall. They know their business. With careful planning, BMW could hit its sales target, and in five years no one would be less happy than they were at this moment. Hitting my five-year target would sustain, in the short run, everything that was good about the business – the UK was a highly profitable country for BMW, it was respected, stable, employed 500 people in the head office and sustained 180 dealers with an average of 30 staff each. Like a great ocean liner, BMW would sail on through good and bad weather.

Steve Nash was Group after-sales director. He'd been at BMW since 1986, and had seen a lot of the company's evolution. He had just completed an interesting project to look at all the resources that BMW had available, and how they could be better used. When he reported to my predecessor, he had to say: "the reason that people don't use the resources well is that they don't know what our strategy is." He remembers:

> "We had been very good at kicking the ball up the field and running after it, but a lot of people had developed their own assumptions about what the right and wrong things to do were, independently of any other part of the business. Looking back, it is amazing that, while we were doing well, it hadn't occurred to anyone at the senior level to stop and ask what we *should* be doing. But no one really thought we needed that at the time. There was a very high-level strategy, but communication from the directors down to the management level was quite poor."

As soon as I had walked into the office, I discovered that there were huge creative opportunities locked up inside BMW's people. It was my habit to manage by walking around, rather than stay in my office and wait for staff to ask to see me. This did not match BMW's existing, more traditional, culture, which generally kept directors away from the staff. (There was even an executive dining room, known in the office as "the goldfish bowl". We changed it into a thinking space for everyone.) I asked my PA to get rid of the sofa that sat outside my office, on which the people who reported to the boss used to sit, obediently waiting to be called in.

Instead, I sorted the massive piles of paper (all emails were routinely printed out) on my desk into folders that I could carry around with me, and spent much of the first month walking from department to department. It became clear that was there was a level of management below my immediate reports who had ideas that would rock the boat, and they were bursting with frustrated energy.

I sensed that the existing culture was stopping these disruptive ideas from being aired. The business was comfortable, and not looking to change. But watching Porsche's great brand slowly sink had shown me that businesses that become complacent are risking everything. When I visited the marketing agencies that worked for BMW it confirmed my fear that the brand had, bit by bit, become a fashion symbol. People were buying the badge, not the world-class engineering, not the exceptional quality, and certainly not the service we offered. The dealer network had become accustomed to making excellent profits and, in many cases, had stopped planning or investing for the future. At my first dealer conference I tortured our dealers by half-seriously threatening to swap the BMW logo in their showroom with the Rover brand. I asked them, would you still be the best dealers in the world if I did? I suspected that we were relying too much on brand, and too little on what we did for our customers. That meant I couldn't succeed unless they were part of my dream too.

In the two decades since that time, I have become a specialist in turning round businesses in trouble, or kickstarting a new era of growth. Again and again, I find businesses making the same mistake.

Like BMW, they all want to secure their future by growing 3% next year.

I cannot count the number of times I have sat in a strategy meeting and heard 3% discussed as if it would be a huge success. Usually, the only people for whom it would be a success would be the managers whose bonuses depended on it. Customers wouldn't notice an improvement. If I backed this 3% solution at BMW, I would commit to keeping the business locked into a path that I didn't believe would build sustained success.

The 3% rule commits you to dream small: you can only achieve 3% by holding most things constant. Revolutionary change is not encouraged. Cutting cost usually dominates the discussion. The 3% rule excludes big dreams by definition.

If you make your 3% target, it may be hailed as a success by board members or shareholders. Day to day, you wouldn't be able to show anyone your success unless you were looking at a spreadsheet. Your team members would tell you their jobs, pay or conditions had not changed. You may be in this position now. What, exactly, are you committed to?

This is also a hidden risk, because this illusion of success means that businesses don't identify the need to change until it is too late. The lack of creative, disruptive thinking becomes a virtue. During times of radical change, when a new competitor, a new idea or a new technology shows up, a 3% target doesn't offer any answers, often because it has usually convinced us to squeeze margins and invest less in innovation.

When the business has to reinvent itself, it may be too late to do anything for precisely these reasons. This may have nothing to do with the quality of the people in the business. *Built to Last*, by Jim Collins and

Jerry Porras,[1] was published in 1994 and identified 18 companies in the world whose values of consistency and steadiness made them bulletproof. Ten years later, seven of those companies had experienced some form of crisis. Size and past success do not protect you for ever. The *Harvard Business Review* reports that 75% of the S&P 500 will change in the next 15 years.[2]

Also, when you try to dream small, the big dreamers in your team will go elsewhere. If they want to create something extraordinary, and that commitment isn't recognized, then they look for something bigger to commit to – and they often find that in their own dreams. Walt Disney walked out of Universal Pictures because it cut his pay; he founded his own animation studio and drew Mickey Mouse. Ross Perot was ignored by his over-cautious superiors at IBM, borrowed $1,000 in 1962 and set up a visionary company called EDS that eventually employed 136,000 people and stole hundreds of IBM's most profitable customers.

In 1996, as I walked around BMW, it was a great business. It was rated by Interbrand, a consultancy that has been measuring the effectiveness of brands for decades, as the 19th most powerful brand in the world, ahead of American Express (20), Chanel (39), Rolex (48) and the BBC (50).[3] Among motor manufacturers, only Mercedes-Benz was considered a more valuable brand. But, in its report that year, Interbrand also sounded a warning that powerful brands were vulnerable because customers were already changing their ideas about quality and service. Cars were becoming less distinctive, as all manufacturers improved the basic product. At a time like this, a commitment to continuity can blind successful companies to their vulnerability, and I worried that the "fashion" for BMW might change. "Newcomers will probably include the automotive sector where differentiation is currently limited, and consumer interest is not sated," Interbrand warned.

I believed my job was precisely to dream bigger, to help BMW to build its future before someone else dreamed it for us, or before our geniuses with bigger dreams walked out the door. So, I started by doing something that BMW UK had never done before: I invited the senior team to think differently, to come with me on a journey to somewhere new and exciting. To share a dream of building something extraordinary.

Early days at BMW on my favourite motorcycle

Shared belief gives us purpose

A sense of purpose, as *New Scientist* magazine recently pointed out,[4] can help to answer the biggest question that we can ask ourselves about our lives and career: "Why am I here?"

We have all asked the same question, and we don't always find an answer. But research has consistently shown that commitment to a goal can help us thrive, and a lack of it can damage us, in every part of our lives.

We all have an example of the problems of commitment. On 31 December every year, according to the University of Scranton, about two out of five of us make a resolution to do something differently next year.[5] About 30% of resolutions last less than a week. Fewer than half of us keep to a resolution for six months, and only 9% achieve a lasting change when we make our commitments according to the calendar.

While many people fail to commit successfully to these goals, 70 years of research clearly shows that experiencing real feelings of purpose has remarkable benefits that do not stop when you leave the office. They are often not even related to the exact commitment you made. "People with a greater sense of purpose live longer, sleep better and have better sex," the *New Scientist* promises, "higher purpose cuts risk of heart disease by 27%, stroke by 22% and Alzheimer's disease by half."

People who find a sense of purpose in their lives also respond more positively to stress: instead of panic or surges of adrenaline, a person who reports high levels of purpose is more likely to activate a part of their brain called the ventral striatum. That's the bit that focuses on what we value most, and allows us to react calmly and focus on the most important problem. The same research shows that commitment to a purpose also helps us work together, because we literally secrete the hormones that encourage it. People who report higher levels of purpose are less distressed in situations when they are in the minority. They find it easier to accept that achieving their aims requires them to get along with other people. These benefits are all free, and you don't need to go to school, have money or have anyone's permission, to get them.

A survey of 205 students in Germany found that we all have the same basic level of commitment.[6] We are equally vulnerable to distractions that undermine it, if we are put into similar situations. But those who are good at commitment simply don't focus on the distraction, and so rarely have that battle of the wills. They take pleasure from completing the job they committed to do, and they focus on that pleasure naturally. Over time, this becomes a habit.

People who demonstrate willpower commit successfully for three reasons, and none of them are based on ability. They take pleasure from seeing through a commitment, it's how they organize every day, and they have learned not to notice distractions.

But you can't change your world in this way by chasing 3%. There's not much pleasure, there's unlikely to be a positive goal to guide your days, and fretting over small changes is likely to mean you are distracted by emails, messages and meaningless meetings.

To unlock the commitment and purpose in a group that has been living with the 3% rule, I have always tried to kick away the assumptions on which that rule was built. When I am working with a new team, I encourage them to forget 3%. What would it take to grow by 30%? And then I make it easier for them: I ask them, what would it take to grow by 300% every year?

The instant response is, of course, we can't do that, because it would mean changing everything. And what, we can then ask, would be the most important thing to change, and how could we change it? And then we give ourselves permission to start to dream.

Back at BMW, I wanted to find our purpose by giving everyone the chance to dream. Not everyone understood the question of what it would take to grow BMW by 300%, but those who did described the world that Interbrand was warning about: drivers would soon stop caring about a product that they were already beginning to think of as a badge, so we needed people to love what we did for them, not just the car that we sold to them.

Our 300% dream became that we would provide world-class service. Instead of thinking about selling 45,000 cars, we wanted to begin a special relationship with 45,000 new drivers. Our job became to create a world-class environment for car drivers to enjoy the product they bought.

It opened the team's minds to doing things differently. World-class service was something we could commit to.

Ultimately, it led to a level of service that meant we made a commitment that, if you ordered parts from us by 4pm, 49 times out of 50 they would be at the dealership by 4am the following morning. The team found a way to do those deliveries through the night, because that's the commitment we made to our dealers and, by extension, to our drivers. The problem we solved wasn't to create a small (or even a large) efficiency in what we did already, because it would not have matched what our customers expected of us. Instead, our dimension for success was to completely rethink how we structured our parts business so that our dealers could fix any car the next day.

But our plan was even bigger. It was no longer about fixing the car's problem, it was about fixing the customer's problem. In an ideal world the customer wants to be scooped up, taken to their appointment or driven home. We had designed the service so that by the time they got home we would have a courtesy car there waiting for them. We recruited 50 customer service people, put them on the road in BMW branded 5 Series Touring model cars, and taught them how to change a wheel and a few more basic repairs; then, if the mechanical problem was harder than that, we told them to pass it to the mechanics. Anything non-mechanical, they should try their best to sort out. The key change was to rethink the issue of a breakdown. We wanted to turn it into an opportunity to deliver a world-class level of service.

Customers sometimes test whether your service really does what it promises. One day a customer was at a petrol station. He had just filled up with fuel and he'd forgotten his wallet, so he called us. We sent a customer service rep to the garage, who paid his bill, shook his hand, thanked him for driving BMW and said, "Have a nice day." That may not have been what we set up the programme to do but, at that moment, it was inspirational service.

Of course, some people at BMW thought I'd gone bonkers. We sold cars, they argued, and anything else was a distraction. If we hit our targets, we would have sold 3% more cars every year for five years. I was challenged by some of my senior colleagues. "Why are you wasting your time with these strategy discussions?" many of them said, "We know who we are." That just encouraged me. I could see that many others intuitively understood what I was trying to do. The excitement was growing.

Sharing belief in change

Not all dreamers are leaders. Leaders use dreams to show how practical change is possible. They help us to understand what we are committing to. The idea of "service" is a concept, and often people think of it as trying a bit harder, without actually changing what you do. But that's just the 3% rule in another form.

The inspirational leaders who understand service, and think about it creatively, change those ideas completely. I always search for better businesses and more able teams, often outside the industry the team I'm leading is working in. Then I'm absolutely unashamed about taking the best examples of service, and using them.

The Ritz-Carlton has always had a radical attitude to providing service.[7] Today we are accustomed to the idea that businesses provide outstanding service as a differentiator. Two decades ago, this was a revelation. At the time I joined BMW, I had previously met one of the people from the Ritz-Carlton group, and was fascinated by its attention to detail, and commitment to what meaningful service would actually be for every guest, rather than the platitudes that some of their rivals used. Service, Ritz-Carlton reasoned, was not about providing a better bowl of fruit in the room, because it looks impressive, but ultimately makes little difference. Instead, when a guest asked for directions, the member of staff would personally escort that person to their destination. When someone had a complaint, the member of staff who heard the complaint would take personal responsibility for it. When someone made a special request, it would be noted, filed and, when the guest stayed in another Ritz-Carlton hotel, fulfilled without them having to ask again. It meant that, coming out of the 1990s recession, the Ritz-Carlton had retained its share of the market without discounting rooms.

This business philosophy had been derived from Japanese total quality management (TQM) theories by a team led by Horst H. Schulze, the Ritz-Carlton's president and chief operating officer. TQM had its origins in manufacturing. It had been developed after the Second World War as a way to help Japanese factories rebuild. One of the principles of TQM is that quality is the responsibility of every employee, and improving the quality of a product or service is something that everyone could, and should, do as part of their job.

At Ritz-Carlton hotels, this wasn't done by bullying the staff. Employees were not hired, they were told they had been "selected". At the time they were told they were "ladies and gentlemen serving ladies and gentlemen". Managers invested more than 100 hours to train each new member of staff, but it was a good investment, because staff turnover was 50% lower than the industry average. This was an unlikely match for my vision of what BMW could become. If we fixed the quality of the service, I reasoned, the sales targets would take care of themselves.

When we were creating our new strategy for BMW, we booked the Hotel Arts in Barcelona for a three-day conference. It was a Ritz-Carlton hotel, and while we were there I asked if we could go backstage with the service team. We saw how they provided service but were not subservient, how their processes worked, how they responded to their guests and how every level of the staff knew, and took ownership of, what they had to do. This was a dream we could believe in.

Steve Nash remembers it now. "The vision of being the most respected and admired service organization was something that people still remembered when I asked them years later. In 2001 it really was something new, looking outside ourselves and our business. It wasn't something we'd done before and it created new thinking" he says.

But how could we provide it? To get to Barcelona, we had bought £50 flights on easyJet. I had also noticed that easyJet was one of the first companies to have a paperless administrative platform, and at BMW we were drowning in paper. It's hard to believe in change when you're just fighting to keep on top of information. I phoned Stelios (now Sir Stelios) Haji-Ioannou, the chief executive.

"My name is Kevin," I said, "I run BMW. Can we come and look at your office?"

Stelios said: "Sure, if I can look at yours."

So that's what we did. We found out how, by having real-time customer information and seat sales data, easyJet could provide revolutionary service to a new category of customers. The service that those customers wanted wasn't about a free glass of champagne or access to a lounge. This new category of customers saw value in a way that existing airlines hadn't planned for, and hadn't dreamed of. The established airlines would take years to catch up, whereas easyJet had dreamed of a different way to do things, and committed to it.

BMW could learn about how to dream from both Ritz-Carlton and easyJet, I argued. Two very different companies had something inspiring in common. Staff at every level committed to a purpose that was bigger and more creative than just getting through the day. The dreams that they shared about how to do it were not fantasies.

They had taken inspirational ideas, and thought through what they meant. They had taken the conventional wisdom of how to run a luxury hotel and a budget airline, and reimagined it by asking "What do our customers need from us?"

Sharing the passion

This is why, although every leader is a dreamer, not every dreamer can be a leader. You might have the idea of how to grow by 300% a year, but that's just the beginning. Ask what this means. What do you have to leave behind? What things do you do every day that hold you back? How can you provide that service at that cost? If you were starting today, what would you build?

When people around you look at the dream and say, "I can be part of shaping that future. I can do that," it's not just a path to a better business, it's an exciting journey, and it's more fun. It's about saying *we can do these things*, and nobody is telling us what we can and can't do.

At BMW, I know I made some people uncomfortable, at every level. But that was my job as a leader, to challenge the old ways of thinking that had been right once. Maybe they weren't going to sustain us in a world which contained Ritz-Carlton and easyJet, but also hundreds of new internet companies that gave consumers control over the service they got and how they received it, and luxury car manufacturers from Japan and South Korea that were targeting BMW.

By 2000 we had sales volumes of 70,000 cars and 2,500 motorcycles, far ahead of the targets I had been given. We had three successive years of record performance. Sales revenues were up 80% and profitability by 500%. But it was not about the numbers. We had created a truly customer-focused organization. I had challenged BMW to think differently, and the people who worked there had responded, and more.

But remember: as in inspiring leader, if you want to challenge the organization to be extraordinary first it has to be *your* dream, and your commitment. This is personal. Which is why, in 2000, I walked out of BMW, and into a startup.

Belief starts with you

When I turned 40 I thought: I don't want to do this any longer. BMW had asked me whether I would be interested to run Japan or the US and I didn't want to do either. I wanted to dream again. One day, just before Christmas 1999, I answered a call from an American entrepreneur called David Geovanis. He told me three things: "We've got a business called CarsDirect. We want to bring it to Europe. We want you to run it."

After Christmas, I was on a plane to Los Angeles. They took me to a warehouse in Culver City. It was a revelation, the first time I saw how the internet would change everything about the way we did business. I saw 600 people selling cars online. I had never seen energy like it. I just thought, this is it. This looks like fun. This looks like an opportunity to create something transformational.

On the other hand, it would mean giving up my lifestyle with one of the world's greatest companies, the support of people around me, and the people I had worked with for the last four years, for a business that didn't exist outside the US, and hadn't existed at all three years ago.

I went home, and I drew a line in my notebook. On the left, I wrote my arguments for staying in BMW. On the right were my reasons for leaving BMW and following my passion for a new challenge. I decided to leave BMW.

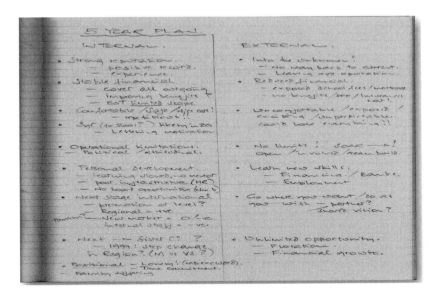

My personal notebook – time to leave BMW and follow my dream

Looking back on it almost two decades later, much of the decision was clearly driven by my dreams. On the left I was worried about politics, finances and my family. Look at the right-hand column. I wanted no limits, to soar into the unknown, but I knew there was no way back if I failed.

Your dream isn't going to be everyone's dream. Some of my colleagues at BMW were going to come with me to CarsDirect but, on the day they were supposed to be leaving, they changed their minds. They realized that it was not their dream. Their dream was different, they followed their path and have been successful in what they have done, and they are still some of my best friends.

If you want to dream, what do you actually want to achieve? Is it more independence, fewer hours, more hours, more money, less money, to see more of your kids? Make a decision, because you only go this way once. If you're a leader, that decision matters. Because if you aren't committed to a dream, you can't inspire others to believe in it.

Notes

1. Collins, J. and Porras, J. 1994. *Built to Last*. New York: HarperBusiness. The companies included that would have not met the criteria for inclusion in the book if it had been written 10 years later were Motorola, Ford, Sony, Walt Disney, Boeing, Nordstrom and Merck. The problems of sustaining success are discussed in this article: Reingold, J. and Underwood, R. 2004. Was "built to last" built to last? *Fast Company*, 88: 103–111.
2. Anthony, S. 2016. What do you really mean by business "transformation"? *Harvard Business Review*, 29 February.
3. Kochan, N. and Interbrand. 1996. *The World's Greatest Brands*. Basingstoke: Palgrave Macmillan UK. My previous employer, Porsche, was 56 places lower, at number 75.
4. Burrell, T. 2017. A meaning to life: how a sense of purpose can keep you healthy, *New Scientist*, 25 January.
5. Statistic Brain Research Institute. 2017. New Year's Resolution Statistics.
6. Resnick, B. 2016. The myth of self-control, *Vox.com*, 24 November.
7. This article from 1993 explains more about a concept that, in the early 1990s when service was often seen as something that was added to a business, rather than being at the centre of it, was truly revolutionary: McDowell, E. 1993. Ritz-Carlton's keys to good service, *New York Times*, 31 March.

Chapter 3

How Good Do You Want to Be?

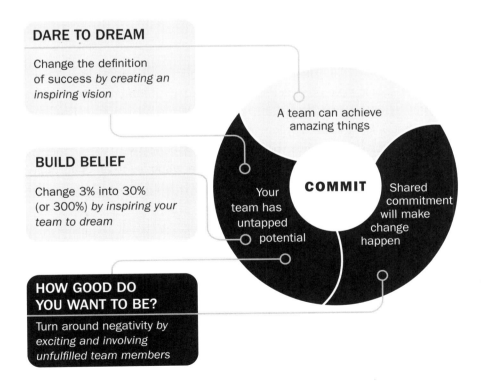

DARE TO DREAM

Change the definition of success *by creating an inspiring vision*

BUILD BELIEF

Change 3% into 30% (or 300%) *by inspiring your team to dream*

HOW GOOD DO YOU WANT TO BE?

Turn around negativity *by exciting and involving unfulfilled team members*

A team can achieve amazing things

COMMIT

Your team has untapped potential

Shared commitment will make change happen

M any companies would wish to have had BMW's problems. It had wonderful products, loyal customers and made a healthy profit. I was attempting to create change from a position of strength.

But this has rarely been the case in my career, and most leaders will find themselves in a turnaround situation at some point in their lives. This will test your ability, your courage, your integrity and your commitment to the limit but, when the stakes are highest, so is the opportunity to do something extraordinary.

In this chapter, I'll explain some of the work I did when I joined a company that should have been doing well, but wasn't. If the process is similar to BMW, the situation certainly was not. But they have one thing in common, something which is especially important for teams that know they are facing challenges. It's not how good you are, it's how good you want to be that matters, because the team's best work is given in response to an opportunity, not in response to a problem.

Why are you here?

Many people would see a difficult situation and choose not to get involved. But, as an inspiring leader, these sort of problems, in which the people in your team are demoralized and vulnerable and have often lost confidence in any kind of leadership, offer a huge opportunity to create something special. To do that you have to be able to raise the heartrate of the business from the moment you get involved. This type of situation emphasizes the difference between being a manager and a leader: remember that a leader keeps his or her eyes on the horizon.

Research shows[1] that leaders who change things tend to behave in four ways (and behave in these ways more often than other people do):

Inspiring leaders don't do it for the money At least, not only for the money. Self-interest is a minor motivation for a transformational leader. They are committed to ideas, goals and dreams.

They look for intellectual stimulation For them, leadership isn't just a job. It is fascinating and energizing.

They have empathy The dream will not be realized at the expense of their team. They understand the people who follow them, and they respect their feelings. Therefore, dreaming is a community activity.

And, most importantly:

Inspiration is their motivation They are not embarrassed or shy about inspiration. Not every day will be happy, and not every project will be a success. But that doesn't extinguish the dream.

Given, not demanded

In 2012 a major bank contacted me and said, "We have an investment, it's got itself into trouble, but we think we could turn this around. Would you look at it for us?" The bank was part owner of the business, alongside a private equity fund, and together they had pumped a little over £20 million into Fairline Boats Limited. The plan was that I would sit on the board, and give advice to the struggling management team, in return for a salary and a small share of the equity. Soon after I agreed to do this the CEO, who was in over his head, left. The Chairman came to see me. It was a problem that they had lost their leader, but "we know who we want to run it," he said.

"Great," I said, "who's that?" And he looked at me and smiled. That's how I found myself living in a house 100 miles from my home, running a luxury boat business that could have been a few weeks away from failing. To be clear: I knew nothing about boats. But I knew a lot about how to turn around struggling businesses, and this was one of those.

Fairline had been founded in 1963 as a family business, and was based in the unlikely setting of Oundle, Northamptonshire, a small town on the River Nene about 40 miles from the coast. Its highly skilled workforce had been hand-building beautiful motor yachts for their wealthy customers in more or less the same way for half a century. The hundreds of people who designed and built the boats were the company's biggest asset, but they needed a successful employer as much as the company needed them: Fairline was also the largest employer by far in the community, and many of its staff had been there all their working lives.

If you had visited when I did, you would have thought the company was doing pretty well. It had a new, modern office 100 metres from its factory. The boats it made had gradually grown as its business expanded, so that the largest under construction was 78ft long – effectively a small floating house, requiring a crew.

I could see immediately that the workforce were proud of what they were doing, but that they clearly regarded their managers as remote and lacking in ideas, which frightened and frustrated them. They were right to be frightened. It was clear that Fairline was heading for a financial iceberg. Management had responded with cuts and repeated rounds of redundancies, which meant that 200 of the 700 staff had lost their jobs in the previous five years. The remaining staff didn't know if they would still have job next year, or even next week. In the recent past they had been working two-day and three-day weeks.

On day two of my new job I went to the factory with the new finance and production directors, who had been there for three and six months.

We wanted to talk to the 500 or so workers who were building the boats. I believed we could save the business, but they didn't know who I was yet, so they had no reason to trust me any more than the last guy. They thought (not unreasonably) that I was just a man from the bank who had been sent to cut costs still further, and (also, not unreasonably) someone who didn't understand anything about their work.

We set up a little speaker and microphone, and I stepped up to it. "Just to be clear, I'm not a banker," I said, "I'm an engineer. My job is to come here and put this business back on its feet, and build something we're proud of."

But when I looked at the faces of people in front of me, I didn't see belief. Arms folded, several of them looked like they wanted to punch me. The rest looked like they wouldn't do much to stop them if it happened.

I had gone to the factory floor to talk to them for ten minutes. When I asked them for their opinions, all their frustration, resentment and lack of trust in the company's leadership came flooding out. I stood there, battered by their complaints, for an hour.

In a situation like this, how do you get people to share your dream? How can you create commitment among people, some of whom would happily toss you into the River Nene? The first step in inspiring leadership is to change yourself by committing to a personal dream. But, unless you can find the way to inspire everyone who you will be leading to share your dream, you won't change anyone, or anything, else.

Inspiring leaders don't just know how commitment works, they know a great deal about how businesses that are driven by commitment succeed. There are three ways in which you may feel committed to your job,[2] which are known as affective, continuance and normative commitment. To translate: the first means you have an emotional attachment to work, the second means it's more hassle to get another job than it is worth, and the third is that someone is telling you that you have to stay.

Only the first one of these can be changed by creating belief and commitment. But that's all you need to create stunning turnarounds, as the team at Fairline would do in the next 14 months.

A vision of the future

This wasn't the first time that this team had heard extravagant dreams about a better future from one of their managers. A sense of purpose may be free, but it's hard to find when all you have had are empty promises, and not all dreamers are leaders.

In my experience, the first practical step to building belief is to find a way to stop arguing about the past, and to start thinking about the future. This isn't easy when you're dealing with resentment, and the only evidence that they have is that leaders don't listen to those problems, or choose not to hear.

Therefore, any dream has to represent something that your team can imagine as real. Often in family or small businesses, that's possible because the dream you want to create is the one that created the business in the first place. It's easy to lose sight of what we wanted to be when we need short-term fixes. I learned that this had happened at Fairline.

When I asked them: "What do we want to be?" they all told me the same thing: "We want to build the best British motor yachts."

That was why they were angry, because they had dedicated their working lives to being the best, creating quality. It's what Fairline used to do, they said, before generations of managers had made a name for themselves by snipping costs out until the business was compromised in so many areas that it didn't work anymore. The cost-cutting, I noticed, hadn't extended to the luxury executive offices the executives had built for themselves next to the factory.

Rebuilding pride in the business would mean rethinking everything about the company's ways of working. But, when we asked the people who built the boats how to make a better future, they knew what had to be done. Encouraging them to imagine a future in which Fairline was the business they wanted it to be gave us a shopping list of the things we could all do. The dream wouldn't be easy, and it wouldn't be a quick fix, and some of it might not even be feasible with the resources we had. But it was, at least, conceivable.

The other advantage to thinking about the future: it was better than the present.

Paint a wall red

We had to show that we heard, and were prepared to act. Often, I've found the best way to inspire belief is to show that you are prepared to back your dream. So, as teams that I work with often do, we painted a wall red.

We didn't *literally* paint a wall. But we demonstrated that our commitment to them was tangible by making a visible change that everybody could see.

During the hour in which the boat-builders complained to me, they mentioned broken promises over bonus pay and wage rates over and over again. Partly this was about their money, because they were supporting families. But also the workers, and their union reps, thought that previous managers had not been straight with them over the payment of bonuses for working hard and well. They felt cheated out of money that was rightfully theirs for the contribution they had made. If you're going to save the company, they said, what are you going to do about our bonuses?

After the meeting, I discussed the fractious atmosphere and the long-running argument about bonuses with my finance and production directors. My finance director said: "Why don't we just fix it tonight?"

At 6pm, I asked my two colleagues what we could do. We locked ourselves in a meeting room with a flip-chart and a spreadsheet, worked out what we could afford to pay, and how we should pay it. At 9.30pm we wrote the new bonus structure on a PowerPoint presentation and went to the pub for a pint. At 7am the next morning, our little show was back in the factory, this time setting up a projector and a screen. When the shift walked in at 8am, we were standing there in the middle of the factory with message that promised "Fairline: the future".

"What are you doing here?" the boat-builders asked.

"You asked us a question last night," I said, "So we've got the answer for you."

At 8.30am we presented their new pay structure. The base salary was far more generous than they had asked for through the union reps. Their productivity bonus was simple: the size of the bonus depended on how many boats they finished. It wasn't based on the quality of their work, because we (rightly, as it turned out) assumed that their pride in the work and desire to build exceptional boats would mean that they took responsibility for it themselves, without us watching over them.

The simple idea of "painting a wall red" is that, if I offered, without preconditions, something meaningful and visible for them, then they knew I was listening to them. When it was based on the dream that I wanted them to share – that we could build the UK's best boats – my commitment made sense. They would also learn that I was prepared to rock the management boat, if that was what was needed.

Painting a wall red was a signal, a way that we could get past a problem that had been lingering for months, a problem that prevented the previous management from making serious progress in restructuring the business. Now we could start to have new conversations about the future, rather than continually arguing about the past. Painting a wall red can be like turning the machine off and on again. It's a visible reboot. Suddenly problems become bumps in the road rather than immovable obstacles. There's always a bump: an inspiring leader will deal with it.

I have never *literally* painted a wall red, though at BMW we managed to remove one that was reducing efficiency in the warehouse. This wall, which served no purpose, had been there for so long that some people had stopped noticing it. That's sometimes the nature of the problems that hold us back – we have forgotten that they can be solved, often quite quickly. There was, for reasons that no one really remembered, a giant wall in the middle of our warehouse that everyone had to walk around, every day. One weekend, we took it down. Afterwards, people asked: what was that wall there for?

Early morning presentation of the new pay deal at Fairline Boats

Integrity is inspiring

Painting a wall red may be a popular idea, but inspiration is not about popularity. Research shows[3] that those of us who worry too much about what other people think find it hardest to maintain commitment to a goal.

If you're going to change the situation, you're going to need to convince sceptical people who don't trust you, don't trust your ideas, or just don't want to change. The way you deal with this will decide whether their commitment ultimately matches (or exceeds) yours.

In my career, I've learned a lot from friends who have a background in the military. They do not have the luxury, in battle, of trying to please people. Therefore, their goal is to achieve the mission and get out alive. The same goes for the elite sportspeople I have worked with. Successful, harmonious teams are not that way because everyone agrees. They encourage open speaking and challenging of objectives, trying to talk frankly about the subject without ever getting personal.

That's why a fundamental principle of the businesses I run is that there is only one version of the truth, which is shared with everyone who shares our belief. Nothing that is not confidential (and there is actually very little information that has to be confidential) should be kept from the people you have asked to believe in the dream, even if the news is bad and uncomfortable. You are in this together.

So if you're going to fall out, fall out early, and then decide what you're going to do about it. At BMW, when one of my directors said he didn't believe in my dream of world-class service as a way to revitalize the company, I offered to help him find another job in a company that suited him. He wasn't a bad person, we just had different ideas, and it was better we were honest at the beginning. Also at BMW, I was lucky that there were plenty of dealers out there who had known me as a kid at Porsche, and didn't feel they had to defer to me. They would never have spoken to my predecessor in the way they spoke to me, but that was a good thing: direct feedback is precious. I could understand their problems better.

You need to inspire everyone, not just the people who already believe you when you walk into the room. And there's no value in anyone in a team who waits until the dream has died, and then says: "I could have told you it wouldn't work."

Gary Klein, a psychologist, specializes in analysing how high-performing teams, such as firefighters or hospital emergency rooms, operate. He has created a technique that he teaches to businesses when they are planning a new project. He calls it a "premortem".[4]

"The premortem technique is a sneaky way to get people to do contrarian, devil's advocate thinking without encountering resistance," he says. "If a project goes poorly, there will be a lessons-learned session that looks at what went wrong and why the project failed – like a medical postmortem. Why don't we do that up front?"

At the planning stage, the team is asked to imagine that they are at the end of the project, and it has failed. He gives them two minutes to write down the reasons. Then they discuss those reasons, and how to make sure they will never happen in real life.

The premortem is a simple device to encourage plain speaking at the time it is most important. By dealing early with problems, the team is more likely to buy into success than if they had pretended that everything was good, or had formed cliques that agreed that whatever you had planned would never work.

One version of the truth means you don't tell your team one set of numbers to make them feel good, and then tell the owners another set. Everyone knows this is what we're doing, and these are the results we're getting. We use one set of measurements, and literally put the results on the wall. We have one plan and one idea to commit to.

At Fairline, there had been at least two versions of the truth, and it hadn't worked. To the workers and the customers, the story was that Fairline was dedicated to quality. Internally, it was trying to squeeze the cost out of the manufacturing process to make it profitable. The people who built the boats knew it. They weren't fools.

We listened to what the workers had to offer, and where the potential growth was, and we said: "If we're going to build the best hand-built motor yachts in the British market, let's focus on quality. We were going to have to manage costs, but first let's support the boat-builders to get the quality right."

It was also a way to show the workers that they didn't have to fight us. When they saw ways that we could improve these boats, we invited them to tell us. Once we had taken the cork out of the bottle, it wasn't going back in.

Inspiring belief

My job is to build successful businesses. Sometimes that is a startup, sometimes it's a re-invigoration of an established company and sometimes it's a turnaround, as with Fairline. Turnarounds are especially challenging but when you build belief and create the culture for success the staff will drive much of the turnaround themselves. Fairline wasn't a balance sheet exercise for me. This was about creating the opportunity for the team to believe again, and then supporting them to rebuild a great company.

We went through hell and back but, 14 months after I walked through the door of Fairline, we were back in profit. Today, some of the guys who would have wanted to punch me in the face the first time we met are still in touch with me with reflections of how much they enjoyed the journey and pride in what we achieved.

In the previous chapter and this one, we have seen that there are four dimensions to belief:

Belief is given, not demanded Your team has the option to not buy into your belief. You can't force them to believe something if you can't convince them. You can ask for it, but very often the first answer may be no.

Belief is about the future One reason why it's hard to build belief is that in everyday life we tend to focus on the past and the present. Your job as a leader is to look to the future. The clarity of your vision will determine whether anyone else is inspired by it too.

Belief needs validation Talk is cheap, and so visible symbols of change and progress give others around you a demonstration that you mean what you say.

Integrity inspires belief Teams cannot believe until they have something to believe in. Too many leaders have multiple versions of the truth. In the businesses that I lead, we have only one.

You can't always choose your team, but they can choose whether to follow you. At BMW, not everyone bought into my dream immediately, but the people working in the business knew they had the backing of the parent company, a profitable balance sheet and job security. Sometimes you are not in that position. When the jobs and livelihoods of your team are under threat, your ability to inspire others to share your commitment will define your chances of success.

I have been through times in business where it's such hard work that you go home and feel like crying. You wonder if you're making progress, and question what it's all about. That's normal. But shared belief will carry you through. Working in a team that shares a dream means that their genius supports you as much as your leadership supports them.

Notes

1. Bernard Bass was the first person to identify this behaviour, but other research shows that it's consistent across all types of business, everywhere in the world. Bass, B. 1985. *Leadership and Performance Beyond Expectations*. New York: Collier Macmillan.
2. Meyer, J. and Meyer, J. 2016. *Handbook of Employee Commitment*. Cheltenham: Edward Elgar Publishing.
3. American Psychological Association. 2012. *What You Need to Know about Willpower: The Psychological Science of Self-control.*
4. He talks at length about this in Kahneman, D. and Klein, G. 2010. Strategic decisions: When can you trust your gut? *McKinsey Quarterly* (March).

Chapter 4

Make the Impossible Possible

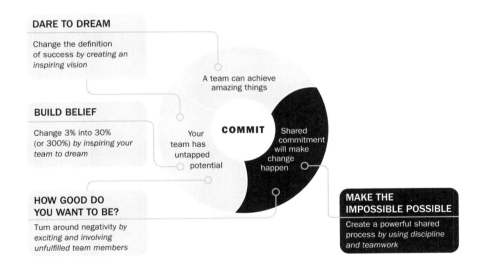

DARE TO DREAM

Change the definition of success *by creating an inspiring vision*

A team can achieve amazing things

BUILD BELIEF

Change 3% into 30% (or 300%) *by inspiring your team to dream*

Your team has untapped potential

COMMIT

Shared commitment will make change happen

HOW GOOD DO YOU WANT TO BE?

Turn around negativity *by exciting and involving unfulfilled team members*

MAKE THE IMPOSSIBLE POSSIBLE

Create a powerful shared process *by using discipline and teamwork*

I believe many limitations that people think they face in life are self-imposed. But how do you break through those limitations?

So far, we have discussed how to dream, and how to connect that dream to the aspirations of your team. But to many of them, especially if the business has struggled, those dreams will seem impossible.

In this chapter, I'm taking apart one of my charity walks to show that something that seemed impossible at first sight wasn't, and that team-work, at its best, can achieve remarkable, apparently impossible, success. Another quote from Muhammad Ali sums it up: "Impossible is not a fact. It's an opinion. Impossible is not a declaration. It's a dare. Impossible is potential."

Realizing that potential, however, does not happen by chance.

Walking to the North Pole

I walked to the North Pole because my sister died of cancer in 2004.

Jayne was 44 years old. After she died, I asked the consultant who had treated her for myeloid leukaemia for five years whether anything would have helped, or if there was a tool that the hospital didn't have that it needed.

"We could do with a monoclonal antibody unit," she said. I asked her to explain, and she told me it was a hospital ward where they treat patients in a specific way, using particular antibodies. I asked why they didn't have one, and then she told me the price of building it. I didn't have that type of money.

My friend Pete Goss, who races yachts, came to see me soon after. Pete is an inspiring person: he became well-known in 1996, when he was sailing in the Vendée Globe, which is a solo race around the world. One of his competitors, Raphaël Dinelli, overturned in a storm. His yacht sank, and he escaped in a life raft. When Pete heard about this, he turned his own boat around, and sailed into the hurricane for two days, eventually finding, and rescuing, Dinelli.[1]

We were doing some work together and he came to speak to one of the teams I was leading. Afterwards he told me that he was thinking of sailing to the North Pole. I asked him how he was going to sail to a place that's covered in ice, and he said on a land yacht, but of course he had to walk there first to check out the terrain.

He said, "It's a bit crazy, but do you want to come?"

When Pete Goss says something's a bit crazy, you know it's true. So I said, "I'd love to."

And then it struck me: that's how I can get the money for the hospital. I will walk to the North Pole, and I'm going to get all the businesspeople I know to sponsor me and donate money.

Walking to the Pole isn't straightforward: you can't just put on a warm hat and head north until you get there. No one got to the Pole at all until 1909, although many people died attempting to do it. It also isn't designed for people in their late 40s who have families and companies to run.

49

But, as we know, ordinary people can do extraordinary things. I did it. You could do it too, if you were committed to achieving it, and knew how to break it down into pieces.

I learned many things about leadership in the two years it took from the day Pete first asked me if I wanted to go to the North Pole, to finally making it. I have used the things I learned in every business I have helped since then. I also went back to the North Pole with Matt, my son, and then to the South Pole, where we became one of the few father-and-son pairs to reach 90 degrees north and south.

And, more importantly, we raised enough money for the North Wales Cancer Treatment Centre to build its monoclonal antibody unit along the way.

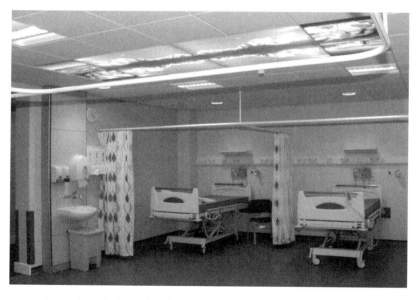

The new eria ward – note the polar pictures set in the ceiling, eria means 'snow' in Welsh

If you want to achieve something inspiring, something that seems impossible when you first have the idea, you will need to work as a team and learn to follow a leader, to rely on the experience and problem-solving of countless experts, and use the tough times to remember why you're doing this crazy thing. Making the impossible possible is a team game, and one in which every detail and discipline matters.

Whatever your impossible dream is, you need to commit from day one, but that's not enough. Making it possible requires five things:

Planning You need to know how you're going to do it. We will talk about planning in detail in the next section of the book. But, if expertise is available, find it.

Preparation Everyone must share the same understanding of what you are about to do. This may be the difference between success and failure.

Support If you do not work together, you will be weak. You need to help each other.

Discipline The plan you make is the plan you execute. In this way you take care of each other.

Teamwork Success depends on the commitment of everyone to a common goal. This, alone, is inspiring.

Planning: if you're not an expert, find one

At this point, I didn't know how to walk to the North Pole, except that it was difficult. But Pete said, "I know this bloke called Alan Chambers who has been there before."

Most people would be happy to admit that we didn't know how to get to the North Pole. But research shows that most of us know far less than we think we do. This is known as "the illusion of explanatory depth". An example: the psychologist Rebecca Lawson[2] asked a group of people to draw a bicycle in a way that would show how it worked. Our first reaction would be: "how hard can that be?" Harder than it seems: about four out of every ten people drew bicycles incorrectly, to the point that they would be impossible to ride.

In everyday life we are part of teams, or lead teams, in which we might casually assume that we know how everything functions. But, if we were asked to describe it in detail, we would have no idea. Even a simple process like the imaginary bicycle in Lawson's experiment: we trust that it works, but we're not sure how. We recognize the bike when we see it, but we wouldn't know where to start if we wanted to build one. If you're a leader who tries to muddle through, your dream will never become reality.

When you want to go to the North Pole, however, there is no alternative but to carefully find out how to do it. Then to work together in a team, and ensure that everyone in that team knows exactly what to do, and how to do it.

In this situation, you couldn't wish for a better leader than Alan Chambers MBE. Among many adventures, Alan had led the first British team to walk unsupported to the North Pole from Canada.[3] The 500 miles took him 70 days on the ice, and he almost died on the way, at one point having to cut his rations down to 100 calories a day. It's a special kind of person who does that and decides that he wants to go back. He had agreed to take Pete, and six more of us, including an accountant, someone who ran a hospital equipment business, and someone whose day job was as part of an airline cabin crew – and, of course, a middle-aged executive. All that we had in common was a dream of reaching the North Pole.

We didn't yet know each other, or what we were letting ourselves in for, when we met in London at the RAF Club. Alan showed us a presentation from his trip in 2000. He didn't try to tell us it would be easy, or avoid the truth. He showed us a slide of him at the beginning, and then a picture of him at the end.

And we thought, "Bloody hell." He looked like a skeleton. The F word was in my mind: I was afraid of what I'd committed to, as any sane person would be. But, as Pete Goss always says, *knowledge dispels fear.*

Alan made us understand exactly what we had let ourselves in for, but he was inspirational too. He would set out for us how much of an adventure, how much fun this was going to be. So, even at the hardest time, he was the leader we all aspire to be, because he made us look forward to the journey.

"Imagine," he would say, "You are going to have the whole world under your feet. You will see a world that most people never have the privilege to see."

Preparation: everyone needs to understand the process

Before you get there, training for the North Pole is all about understanding the process. How do you train to walk for weeks when it's 40 below zero, when polar bears can kill you even if exhaustion or hypothermia does not? The truth is, you can't. But we got as close as we could. Alan took a bunch of raw recruits, and had to whip us into shape to survive in one of the most hostile environments on Earth. The next months would be a process of using that knowledge to make the dream possible, and get home safely.

We learned that, at the Pole, you can't sit and wait for help, because none is coming, so we had to solve our own problems. First of all, we all had to be fit enough to cope. Alan and Pete organized training events where we'd trek around the Brecon Beacons, in South Wales, dragging tyres behind us, to simulate dragging our kit. When I was halfway up a mountain, in the rain, strapped to a tyre, so tired that I just wanted to go home and get warm, I would already be thinking: I don't want to let the team down. There was a lot of cycling. I was averagely fit, but this was a different level of commitment and stamina.

When it hurts, you can remind yourself why you're there. Under that kind of stress, the commitment you made to six strangers, and a hospital in Wales, means that you can come together as a team.

You can get to a certain level of fitness by training every day. (I still go out in the morning, and drag tyres around in the woods near my house. It turns out that it's a surprisingly hard habit to break). But preparation also means understanding what you will be working with, in detail. In any task, understanding the limitations that the environment puts on you, and how you use your equipment to beat it, is vital for survival, either as a business or – this time – literally.

For example, we would sleep in three tents that we would have to put up every day when we stopped. If you have ever tried to put up a tent when you're tired, or maybe when it is a bit windy, and get your sleeping bag inside, you know that it can take hours. We weren't going to have that sort of time on the Polar ice cap after walking in minus 40°C for 12 hours. We might be putting up a tent in 50 knots of wind, and you don't carry a spare if this one blows away.

When you can put up that tent, you also need to learn how to protect it from a storm. That means learning how to build a wall of ice blocks to protect the tent every night. You need to know how to use the burners safely to melt snow to make water, because every day we would need to drink a minimum of three litres of fluid each, and there's no fresh water, at least none in liquid form, in the Arctic Circle.

Detailed preparation for us meant doing the same things again and again, looking at every detail, never trusting to luck. It was never easy, but that's not the point. The point was, when we set out on the first day, we had the confidence that, as a team, we knew how to make it.

Support: you can't do it on your own

As a leader, you can set an example, you can never let your team down, but you can't do *everything*. You need to trust, and rely on, the expertise of those around you. If you are setting out into the unknown, it might be an alien landscape for you. But that's when you value the people who have been there before you. People who can say: I've got this.

Logistically, getting to the point where you start walking towards the North Pole isn't straightforward. You, your team and your kit eventually arrive in a town on an island at the top of Norway called Longyearbyen ("Long year town", because it never gets dark in summer at the pole), which is one of the stranger places on Earth. It's the northernmost town in the world, is surrounded by 3,000 polar bears (more than the human population), and visitors are officially discouraged from dying there (the bodies do not decompose, so the graveyard is full).

When the conditions are right, you fly another three hours on to Camp Barneo, which is a camp set up every year on the ice cap. Because the Polar ice floats on ocean, every year Barneo is in a different place. The Polar ice cap is simply frozen ocean – 2 metres of ice floating on 2,000 metres of water – and, as the ice cap moves, every day it's in a different place too. To create the runway there, once a year a Russian team flies there and parachutes a bulldozer and a driver out the back of an aeroplane. He cuts a flat track in the snow so that the aeroplane can land, and every year when the ice melts, the bulldozer drops through the ice. The bed of the Arctic Ocean is gradually filling up with Russian bulldozers.

Once the runway is established, Base Camp Barneo can be built. It is a tented village, consisting of ten tents, and a couple of helicopters. It is the biggest camp for more than 1,000 miles in any direction. For the aeroplanes and teams arriving later the runway is marked with black bin bags full of snow. On approach the pilot flies around looking for the runway, because the ice cap will have moved since the last time he was there. Occasionally, the ice will crack and the runway will break in half. Then you'll see somebody with a hosepipe trying to put hot water on it to reseal it.

The point is: in a place like this, you realize that experience of the conditions saves lives. When you explore, technology will help you to a point – but many jobs aren't done with sophisticated instruments and computers. It makes you aware how much, every day, we rely on the collective judgement and experience of people in the team who know exactly what they are doing.

So, on day one of our Polar trek, all the teams who would be walking on the ice cap squeezed into one military helicopter. Ours was packed with 30 people, two dog sleds, 10 dogs and everyone's gear. There were, needless to say, no seats. On the floor right next to my feet, there was a mysterious car wheel, which was out of place considering there were no cars for hundreds of miles. When we were six metres off the ground, one of the crew picked up this car wheel, leaned out of the helicopter, and dropped it on the ice. If it bounced, you could land a helicopter.

About a metre off the ground, one of the crew would jump out of the helicopter and guide it down. A pilot landing a very heavy, overloaded helicopter on a featureless sheet of ice has no idea how far away it is, or whether the ice will take the weight of the helicopter, because ice looks more or less the same from any distance. The last thing you want to do is crack the ice and sink the helicopter.

As we hovered, wheels barely touching the ice, we bundled out, pulled our kit together, and watched as the rotors picked up speed. We were showered with chunks of ice as we watched our last link with civilization disappear.

Silence.

We put on our sledge harnesses, as we were trained to do, and started walking.

Discipline: we take care of each other

The sledge we each pulled behind us is called a pulk. It is made of plastic, and it looks like a neon bathtub. Inside this, we would put a huge nylon bag in which we packed our clothes, our food, the tents, our tools, our bedding – everything we needed for the time we spent on the ice. In the front, you have your big gloves and your big coat. Underneath them, your flasks. Underneath that, your day snacks, and then you work backwards. Alan had repeatedly drummed into us: pack the same gear, the same way, on every sledge.

Why do this? Because in an emergency, if someone falls through the ice, we needed to know immediately where his spare clothes are, where the sleeping bag is and where the food and batteries are kept. This was a team effort, and a team effort required discipline. Our vision of success was that we were all going get to the Pole and get home safely. Our first responsibility was to be a part of the team. And that meant we committed to live by those standards.

One day, Alan had found that one of our team wasn't packing his gear correctly. "That's not a kit," he said, "that's a f***ing vortex." It was a danger to him, and it did not help the team. Before anyone moved, Alan made him take out everything and repack it properly.

We had trained for the cold but, when you first set foot on the Polar ice cap, it's still a shock. The first time I stepped out of the plane I felt as if somebody had hit me in the face with a baseball bat. It was shockingly cold. One person who had flown up with us to join another expedition got off the flight at Camp Barneo, got straight back on the plane, and flew home. After all that training, she just couldn't face it.

The ice cap is shockingly cold, but also shockingly open, and shockingly big. In these situations, you can easily lose sight of what you are meant to do, and what your role is. Anyone can stay calm when it doesn't matter, but it's harder to maintain your discipline at a time like this. That discipline has stayed with me, and I think about it every day. You look after your kit, and your kit will look after you.

Don't carry baggage

Everything you take, you have to drag. Somebody packed a pair of snowshoes, which weren't part of our agreed kit. Alan said, "You know what those things weigh? Two kilos. Get rid of them." The reason is that they aren't just two kilos today, they are two kilos every day. Packing "just in case" always seems like it's a good idea until you have to pull it behind you for weeks. On another trip, he had found that one of the expeditioners had, in secret, added lots of spare kit. He pulled the contraband out, dug a hole in the ground, and set fire to it.

We all like to carry baggage that ultimately just slows us down: we make a plan, we decide exactly what we need, and agree it with others – and then we add a bit extra that distracts us and holds us back. We literally dragged our baggage with us for 12 hours a day, over lumps of ice the size of a house, for days on end. It showed us, in the clearest way possible, that the difference between achieving the impossible and just falling short could have been that extra pair of snowshoes. We were in an extreme environment, and we needed to focus on extreme details.

Everyone knows their job

At the end of the day you are tired, but you each have a different job. Two people set the tents up. Somebody else's job is to get the bedding inside and then light the stove, without burning the tent, and begin melting ice. Another team member will be cutting ice blocks for the melting pot. We all want a hot drink, but it will take an hour to melt the snow. The longer you stand around talking, or deciding who does what, the longer it will be until you get that drink.

In my experience, leadership isn't about telling people what to do, it's about creating a situation in which people understand what to do and why they are doing it, and letting them get on with it.

Every minute counts

Each day we would walk for exactly an hour and then stop for 10 minutes. One person's job was to measure that 10 minutes precisely, and call out when nine minutes had elapsed. Imagine the situation: we all stop walking, open the front of our sledges and put on our big coats and big gloves, take out our flask for a drink, and our day snacks to take in some of the 7,000 calories we needed to eat every day. When we were setting off again, it would take one minute to take the coat and gloves off and pack them up. It's 40° below zero: you can't put anyone in the situation in which they are stripped off, zipped up and ready to go, while you're still sitting there with a cup of tea. Team responsibility and discipline is the key to making the most of your time and to maintaining a healthy and positive team spirit.

Sometimes I meet leaders who, for some reason, have little sense of urgency, no matter how extreme the situation. They confuse relaxation with a lack of priority. For example, when cashflow is a problem, it's not a case of how much money you can get by the end of the month, it's how much you can find by Friday when you need to pay staff. When we need to make a difficult decision, I don't want you to call me back in the morning. I need to speak to you now. You owe it to the team to make that call. That is the same team responsibility in business.

Every detail is important

On the Polar ice cap, I learned from Alan that you never leave a zip undone. If you simply drop a glove, you can have a serious problem. The dream only becomes reality when a thousand tiny, automatic actions every day are done correctly, every day, by everyone. Even today, I have the habit of doing up a zip that I see undone. In the same way, when I'm in the office, I never walk past a problem and assume someone else will fix it, or leave a piece of litter for the cleaners.

No a'holes at the poles

You get friction when people get physically and emotionally stressed. But you must be open to criticism when you're pushing to achieve something this difficult. Every night on the ice, we would sleep in different groups. We had a team of seven: two would sleep in one tent, two in another and three in the other. Mixing the groups up meant that, no matter how stressful the day had been, we never created cliques.

Stress and tiredness can produce some unexpected reactions. When we were at home, one of our group never had a doubt in his mind that he was going to get to the Pole. Part of the way into our trek, he sat down on the ice and said, "That's it, I'm done. I can't go any further."

Alan chatted quietly to him for a while, but he wasn't budging. In the end, he said: "We've got two guns. I'll leave you one. We'll pick you up on the way back. See you in two weeks."

That got him up. And, a week later, he made it. In those extreme situations, a leader has to be the person that says, "You are hurting the group."

Alan's motto was: "No a'holes at the poles." He interviewed us before he let us on the team, and, if he had any doubts at that time, we wouldn't have made it. It didn't matter how much we wanted to be there, he couldn't allow anyone to damage the group. As the leader, it's uncomfortable when you know that someone is damaging the team, and will continue to undermine it as long as they are part of it. But, as Alan knew, your first responsibility is to make sure your team works. It is not to make everyone happy in that team, all the time.

In my experience, everyone has a bad day, but truly destructive people are rare. On the other hand, these people will be devastating to the team's commitment. When you try to make the impossible possible, they are the ones who will hold you back by reminding everyone not how far you've come, but how far you have to go, and how unlikely it is that you will make it (even if that's not true). I call them "Energy vampires". There is no other way to deal with them but to exclude them from the situation. It's hard to do in the Arctic Circle. At work, you need to help them to find something else to do, quickly.

Accept setbacks, and try again

From time to time, you will have that bad day. After walking to the North and South Poles, I went back to the Arctic with my son when he was 21 years old, with Alan Chambers leading the expedition again. We got within half a mile of the North Pole and suddenly, in front of us, there was water. We walked a mile one way, and couldn't get across. We walked a mile the other way, and we couldn't get across. So we came back to the narrowest part and built a bridge by finding lumps of ice, and throwing them into the water. We spent three hours to create something that we could ski across, watching all the time for bears.

We finished the bridge and Alan said, "I'll go across first and I'll test it." And just as he was about to try, the whole floe just moved apart. Our ice bridge just floated away.

Sometimes, you need to know when to stop for the day. We were tired, impatient to get there and much more likely to make a fatal error if we tried again. The calm thing to do wasn't to build another bridge, or panic, or blame each other. It was to set up camp, sleep, come back the next day and start again. We had to wait one more day to get to the Pole, but we made it safely. You can't beat nature.

Teamwork: working together is an extraordinary experience

On the satphone the Russians had told us when they would have a helicopter passing the North Pole, to take us back to Camp Barneo. We really had to rush to make it, as this was one flight we couldn't afford to miss. One night we had three hours' sleep and then we set off again walking 21 hours out of 24.

We got to the North Pole on time, on 26 April 2006, at 6:50am.

Somebody confessed that they'd secretly packed a bottle of champagne. This seemed like a good idea until they tried to open it. It was, of course, frozen solid. Somebody else had brought some bacon and some buns. We were going to have a bacon sandwich, but what can you do with a frozen lump of bacon? So we cancelled our champagne reception and phoned the Russians and said, "We're here."

And they said, "Sorry. We won't be there until tomorrow." We squashed into two tents, and fell into a deep, exhausted sleep. I was dreaming I was in a violent storm. And then I woke up, and realized the storm was the helicopter which had just landed next to us. Always expect the unexpected.

When you go through a test that is both physically and emotionally extreme you become very close to the people who go through it with you, and you appreciate that, to make the impossible possible, you can't do it without them and the small things really matter. You are constantly dealing with obstacles, breaking them down into manageable pieces. There's a little win in getting over that lump of ice. A little win in getting across that rubble field.

Even though everyone contributes, somebody has to be the leader. Because in difficult situations, when people are uncomfortable, and tired and hungry and grumpy, if somebody isn't absolutely clear about next steps your inspired team can quickly fall apart.

But what a great situation to be in! You are the person who, when everything could fail, finds that way through. My job in business is to say to established teams, "let's pretend that we don't know the limitations that we know". I have found that the limitations I thought I had in business were mostly self-imposed.

Commitment to achieving a dream in others is always inspiring. I have been lucky enough to work with Professor Charles Elachi, the head of the NASA project to land the Curiosity rover on Mars. Previous exploration devices that had landed on Mars were the size of a large dog. Curiosity is the size of an SUV, has a mass of 899kg, and had to travel 560 million km in eight months before being deposited safely on the planet in 2012. Of course, they had never done anything like it before, no one had. Many of his colleagues told him it was impossible. His reply: "The only thing that is impossible is defeating the laws of physics. Everything else is possible." And, sure enough, they solved the problem.

Transcend your self-imposed limitations

Most of the time pushing past your self-imposed limitations is scary, but using planning, preparation, support, discipline and teamwork to transcend them isn't rocket science. Although, in Charles' case, it was.

NASA's remarkable dreamers like Professor Elachi and his team successfully achieve things that most of us would dismiss as impossible. As President John F. Kennedy said in 1962 when he first committed the US to landing a man on the moon: "We choose to go to the Moon in this decade and do the other things, not because they are easy, but because they are hard; because that goal will serve to organize and measure the best of our energies and skills."

In our mission Alan Chambers was, and is, an incredibly inspirational leader. I tell my teams about our adventure, and say: "When we're setting out to achieve the next level, we're going for *our* North Pole." And, just like our adventure, people get tired along the way, and sometimes lose their discipline. Strong people say they can't go any further because they can't quite see where the end is. We get stressed, and argue, and form cliques.

At that point, my job – and your job – is to be the inspirational leader that Alan Chambers was for us. You will all get through this, I tell them. What do you want them to do? The first thing you want them to do is to be there again tomorrow, remembering the commitment we made when we had this dream. Just come in with the right attitude in the morning, and solve the next problem, in the way we said we would. Just show up. Because that goes a long way towards making the impossible happen.

Then, as Alan used to tell us, we will be standing on top of the world.

Kevin Gaskell, Alan Chambers MBE, Matt Gaskell standing at the north pole

Notes

1. You can read more about this inspiring story in Goss, P. 1998. *Close to the Wind: An Extraordinary Story of Triumph Over Adversity*. London: Headline.
2. Lawson, R. 2006. The science of cycology: Failures to understand how everyday objects work, *Memory & Cognition*, 34(8): 1667–1675.
3. You can find out more about how he survived in the book he wrote with Dr Richard Hale: Chambers, A. and Hale, R. 2009. *Keep Walking: Leadership Learning in Action*. London: MX Publishing.

Chapter 5

Confront the F Word

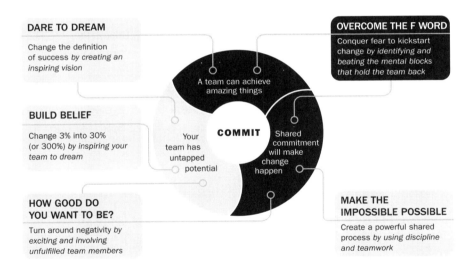

DARE TO DREAM

Change the definition of success *by creating an inspiring vision*

BUILD BELIEF

Change 3% into 30% (or 300%) *by inspiring your team to dream*

HOW GOOD DO YOU WANT TO BE?

Turn around negativity *by exciting and involving unfulfilled team members*

A team can achieve amazing things

COMMIT

Your team has untapped potential

Shared commitment will make change happen

OVERCOME THE F WORD

Conquer fear to kickstart change *by identifying and beating the mental blocks that hold the team back*

MAKE THE IMPOSSIBLE POSSIBLE

Create a powerful shared process *by using discipline and teamwork*

A chieving a dream. Making the impossible possible. Asking how good you want to be. Some of you will be filled with excitement at the idea of doing things like this. This might be why you want to be a leader. Some of you will feel panic about the idea of launching into the unknown. If this is you, you are not alone. All of us are held back by our fears.

The most obvious fear is that you will fail. But there are others. Fear of looking ridiculous. Fear of rejection. Fear that people will not follow you.

The final part of commitment is the commitment to break through those fears as a team. Fear is natural, but living in fear is not. Everyone is afraid sometimes. It's what you, and your team, do about that fear that matters.

Fear of flying

A man, in his 50s, is sitting in the doorway of a plane like a condemned man. Below him, 13,500 feet away, is a patchwork of fields, a coastline, the sea. It all looks so small.

He is terrified. He holds on to the doorway, because that reminds him of the certain world that's two-and-a-half-miles below. He knows that everyone is waiting for him to step out, but he's scared of heights: he got dizzy when he was given a room on the eighth floor of a hotel. As he looks down, he knows there are two instructors to hold on to him, and keep him safe.

That doesn't matter right now, because his instincts tell him that when he throws himself out of that doorway he will fall to his death.

His son is by the door, wearing a helmet with the visor pushed up. He says, "Hey, what's the worst that can happen?", and then tumbles out. The man watches him disappear. He thinks: I've just watched my son kill himself.

But, of course, he hasn't. His son has a parachute, and the man also has a parachute. Actually, a parachute, and a spare. And a team of people around him who know what to do. He lets himself go, and then he is falling. He doesn't need anyone to nag him, or encourage him, or hold his hand, because it is exhilarating to just fly. As he plunges towards the Earth at 122mph, waiting for his parachute to open, he can relax for the first time in a sleepless week.

The man, of course, was me. Heights scare me stiff, but both my kids are keen skydivers, and it was them who dragged me along. I was

The frightened flyer starts to enjoy flying

terrified before I went out of the plane but after I fell 13,500 feet for the first time, I wanted to do it again, and again. It's the same when you change your business. You stand on the edge and you look, and you think of all the reasons why not. The fear of failure is kind of the fear of the unknown. It's the fear of suddenly having to think: what's going to happen?

Fear of losing

When I talk about the "F word", some people assume that I'm telling people not to worry about failing. It's true that we can't rule out failure, because when we set out, we don't know exactly what's in front of us (and, even if we did, it's constantly changing). I have had many failures, but I always got back up, and tried again.

But the F word that teams I work with must confront comes before that: it's Fear. Commitment to lead change can be frightening, because we have decided to do things differently, to throw away the old certainties that hold us back, and to be different. I often work with people who will never get as far as risking failure, because they are afraid to make the change – even if they know, deep inside, that might condemn them to a different type of failure: a slow, inevitable, unstoppable decline.

The psychologist Daniel Kahneman describes a simple experiment[1] that shows how we prefer to hang on to what we have. He gave a mug to half the participants in an experiment, and asked them to name a selling price. The others, who hadn't been given the mug, had to name a buying price. If the selling price matched the buying price, the deal was done.

Surprisingly, buyers consistently offer amounts about half of what the sellers are willing to take. This effect is common across all sorts of similar experiments. When we have something, we instinctively value it more highly.

Kahneman compares this "loss aversion" to a baby clinging on to its toy. But it also makes us cling on to jobs we don't like, ways of doing things that we could improve or business relationships that need to change. To break out of a "loss aversion" mentality, we need to commit wholeheartedly to a new way of operating. Inspiring leadership means that when we commit, we commit fully, and immediately. We may be afraid, but we do it together as a team.

Fear of creative destruction

There's a quote that you will often hear: "It is not the strongest of the species, nor the most intelligent that survives. It is the one that is most adaptable to change."[2]

The people that trot out this quote are often good test cases: often businesses that I deal with are happy to talk about change, or put this quote in their presentations, but have become lost in fiddling with the business. This is the 3% rule again, it isn't the sort of change that could save a business. If you're truly scared of heights, jumping off a box might seem more impressive to you than to anyone else.

But it's not a question of what seems impressive to you. Sometimes we all have to jump out of the aeroplane. Businesses grow in stages, and what made you successful in the first stage probably won't make you successful in the second or the third stage, because the world moves on. Technology changes. The law changes. Your competitive marketplace changes. Your customers' expectations change.

We are accustomed to viewing these changes as a smooth process of adjustment. Joseph Schumpeter,[3] an Austrian economist who was active in the first half of the 20th century, was the first to disagree. He saw a world in which businesses would innovate, and grow successful, and be copied by others, and gradually improved, and would all make money. Schumpeter was the first to realize how important the entrepreneurs were, because they created new, different ways to do the same thing. People who think differently suddenly grab a part of the market because their products are cheaper, better or easier to use, and the businesses that became complacent cannot compete. They were growing slowly, but they fail quickly.

Schumpeter called this process "creative destruction". It's often used by technology companies, because it seems to fit the image of Silicon Valley, but it is just as relevant to other types of business, as long as there is some opportunity to change.

It can, however, be hard to drive this process from within. To do that, you first need to identify when you need to employ creative destruction. It can be hard to realize that the magic that got you to this point no longer works. At Porsche, we looked hard at our strengths: they should have been quality, engineering, design, integrity and racing heritage. But, when we looked at the cars we made, we had stopped noticing the simple things that had begun to drive customers crazy, and were damaging our business because we were too timid to change them. For example, they were no longer prepared to put up with a leaky, squeaky roof, just because it was a traditional Porsche roof. It was cool in the 1950s. But we weren't in the 1950s any more.

Fear of the first step

As an inspiring leader, you have to get your team to take that step, even though you're just as afraid as they are. When I'm working with a new team, I will say to them: "Trust me. I've been here before. I've jumped out of this plane before, you're not going to die."

It is essential to make sure that everyone takes this step because, until they do, they will hold you back. Once you are moving, the fear goes away, because you're focusing on the journey, and you can learn to trust the process, because you're on the inside of it – remember, we don't jump without a clear vision of success, this is what helps us to stop obsessing about what we are leaving behind.

But this isn't to say that everyone will feel comfortable. If it's all under control, I'd argue that you're not moving fast enough. Often we obsess about measuring every key performance indicator, compiling dashboards, using last year's or last month's accounts to measure how well we are doing. Although the change you will create is exhaustively planned and managed (we will go into that in more detail later), you should be inspiring your team to become excited about the future, not about measuring history.

When you look forward to flying, you can start looking at your business in a different way. It's easier to start looking at the scary places and think: "We could do something about that."

On the other hand, this doesn't happen easily. There are several common objections based on fear that you might have heard (or even made) in the past.

"We're too busy to change"

Recently I worked with a small business run by Nicola, a smart, dynamic, successful entrepreneur who runs a company called Xcel Sales Ltd.

Her business idea is simple: if you want to sell something, we find sales leads. Not lists of emails, or people who have filled in a form, but high-quality, effective leads that point to people who want to buy your product, for which the asking price per lead is several hundred pounds. It's a high-skill business which relies upon quality staff.

When we met, she was about to drive herself out of business, because she had been too successful. As she expanded and took on new staff, her costs had ballooned, and cashflow had become a problem. This is not unusual – CB Insights research[4] shows that, apart from having a product that no one wanted (which she emphatically did not), it's the most common reason that startups fail, helping to cause 29% of failures.

But Nicola was losing money on every deal she did. Her natural reaction was to work harder, and take on more work. Some people are so committed to working harder, they don't think about working smarter. Talented people like her never stop. As long as she was running faster, working all hours, she didn't need to face the fear that she had to change the way she ran her business.

So the first thing we did was stop. Instead of piling in the work, we took some time to think. Soon we realized that, for some customers, she was providing an excellent service, and selling it too cheap. For others, many of which she had been winning to bring in cash, she could provide a different, lower-priced product with less service (or, indeed, increase the chances her business would survive by ceasing to do business with them). Also, she needed to change her payment terms.

Nicola committed to making the change. In 100 days, she went from a business that was losing large amounts of cash to one that was breaking even, and which was well-set to grow quickly, and profitably, in the next 1,000 days.

My advice wasn't incredibly profound but sometimes, when we are "too busy" to think about the future, it's our fear that locks us into constant activity. Until we stop doing the things that are making us fail, we can't commit to the changes that will help us succeed.

Nicola said to me: "You've allowed me to think about my business again, and focus on what I'm good at." Which is why she is going to succeed. She has so many smart ideas, but the paralysing fear of running a business that was running out of cash was stopping her from using them. If this is your team, sooner or later you will have to face the fear. When I jumped out of the aeroplane, I could have chickened out, stayed in the plane, landed on the airstrip and gone out to dinner. But in business you might be faced with a different problem: you can let fear decide your actions, stay on the aeroplane, but sometimes the aeroplane's only got another 10 minutes of fuel in it. You will be caught in the creative destruction.

Even if you're running a stable business, you might be closer to that scenario than you think. It's comfortable to say that you're too busy to sit down with your team and ask why you are not growing at 30% per annum but, if you don't do that, maybe that's not because you are too busy to make it a priority. Perhaps a part of you, like most of us, is afraid of heights.

"We're too big to change"

I hear it all the time when I meet leaders who want to do better, but don't want to commit to a different future. "But we're too big to change," they tell me, as if there's some special law.

As layers of management – and departments and offices – expand, it becomes hard to be a brave, inspiring leader. There are many more personalities, many more day-to-day problems to distract you. There's the constant idea that the most important job that a leader can do is to cut costs, not rebuild the company. Companies become run by consultants, who may be smart but can also strangle the organization with rules.

Being "too big to change" often translates into a different fear: the fear of speaking truth to power, or the fear of breaking rules.

For example, I was consulting for a large customer-facing organization recently. The head of department I was speaking to told me that she was about to outsource an important part of the business overseas.

Me: "I've been through it twice and it may be cheap, but the quality will go down and your business will suffer. I know a company here that can do exactly what you need, has an installed user base that you can reference, will work at a much lower cost, and you won't have to go through international outsourcing."

Her: "That would have been interesting, but we closed the tender last Thursday."

Me: "You're seriously telling me you're going to compromise your business because of an arbitrary date on a tender?"

Her: "Yes."

Now one year and £30 million later, the company has lost control of the project. It is suffering. The customers are disappointed with quality and their competitors are closing in. But it is not all bad news. They closed the tender on time.

A healthy disregard for the "impossible" (in this case, impossible is an exaggeration) is still an asset in a large business. This is confidence, determination and commitment to do something that helps the company, not bravery.

I also hear "I just run a division." My advice: improve your division. You'll never meet a boss who will complain at you because your division has improved.

"We don't do it like that around here"

At Porsche, we changed the structure of the business. We had 13 divisions before the change, and 5 after it. My colleagues considered that it was extraordinary at the time, but my question to them was: why do we have 13 divisions?

The answer was, we always have had 13 divisions. That was, 13 silos of information which we didn't need. If we had been starting the company from scratch, we wouldn't have created 13 divisions.

"Not doing it like that" may be a deep-rooted manifestation of fear of change, but it's a hard one to beat. Clay Christensen is the person who invented the term "disruptive innovation" in the 1990s. His idea, which can be traced back to Schumpeter, is that businesses protect their most profitable products by improving them a little every year. They don't invest in big, radical new ideas, because they have a sustainable business to protect. The disruptive innovation comes from outside the business: someone has a new idea (they might have even left the dominant company because they have a new idea), which is radically better or cheaper. At first, only a small number of customers are interested, and so the dominant company ignores it, because that's not the way it does things. By the time the disruptive new technology becomes more popular (PCs replace giant computers, digital cameras replace film, or Wikipedia replaces 20-volume encyclopedias), it's too late for the established company to change.

The simple way to avoid this, you'd think, is to lead your own programme of disruptive innovation, from inside. But Christensen points out[5] that it isn't that simple:

"It's no wonder that innovation is so difficult for established firms. They employ highly capable people – and then set them to work within processes and business models that doom them to failure."

His argument is that success decreases the possibility of change. Businesses have resources: people, buildings and relationships. On top of those, they build processes, which are designed not to change, and they employ managers for their ability to keep those processes consistent. On top of those processes they have a layer of values, which might not even be written down, but determine the way we think about deciding what's possible.

If you're going to be an inspiring leader, it's not just about fixing things that everyone knows to be wrong. Sometimes you will have to lead change when no one else has seen the need to do it yet, because your ideas challenge their values, disrupt their processes and might change their resources. As in Kahneman's experiment, they might fear that you're taking something away from them, rather than building something extraordinary. They fear the destruction rather than loving the creative part, and may instinctively block change.

How can we deal with this prevarication? Recent research shows[6] that sharing commitment has a big effect on fear. We all share some fear about the future, and the amount of that fear predicts how likely we are to procrastinate. But when we feel competent about what we should be doing, and a sense of autonomy, we just get on with it. I didn't jump out of the aeroplane because I was told to. I did it because I had confidence in the people around me and a clear idea that it would be amazing. Both of which were correct.

The whinge wall

How, then, can we overcome fear by creating that sense of autonomy? I've been on some team-building sessions, but I don't often choose to take a team away and build a raft. Instead, we talk honestly about what we need to do. Hence the tool I call the whinge wall.

At Fairline we had a lot of plywood, because we used it to build boats. Imagine a sheet of plywood, four feet by eight, with paper stuck on it. We write in big letters, on the top, "Whinge wall". We have another similar board, on which we write "Ideas wall". We will use this later.

Every business has moans and grumbles. The role of an inspiring leader is not to pretend they don't exist, it's to deal with them. When we talk about the problems we face and how we should change for the better I ask them to write their whinge on the wall. Everything is possible, we don't discuss budgets (or resources or processes). I usually prefer a large group of 30 to 50 drawn from right across the business, rather than just a few executives. For the first two hours, nobody writes anything, and then one brave person gets up, walks to the wall and writes down a whinge. By the end of the two days, the wall will be covered.

But then we do not start to pick off the whinges, one by one, because that won't change much. This is a trigger to say, "How are we going to transform this business *so that those problems go away naturally*?"

Those ideas go on the ideas wall. This is the beginning of the process of building a 1,000-day plan for success and will be the focus of the next section. The final thing we do is to check that everything on the whinge wall is covered. Every single whinge.

The whinge wall starts to fill with opportunities for improvement

"We're too busy to change", "We're too big to change", "We don't do it like that around here": the whinge wall is a way to confront the fear of change. I know it's comfortable to come into work every day, sit in the same chair, do the same thing and get paid at the end of the month. Actually, inside, nagging away at you, is the fear the business is going to flatline, or be undercut by someone else, or is going to change in ways you don't have control over, and then you're going to lose your job.

How are you going to work together to transform this business to build something extraordinary, so none of you lose your job? The whinge wall holds up a mirror to our uncomfortable fears.

Notes

1. You can read about it in Kahneman, D. 2011. *Thinking, Fast and Slow*. New York: Farrar, Straus and Giroux.
2. Often attributed to Charles Darwin.
3. Schumpeter had three ambitions, he claimed: to be the greatest lover in Vienna, the best horseman in Europe and the world's greatest economist. He didn't succeed, he added, only because of the decline of the cavalry.
4. CB Insights. 2017. *The Top 20 Reasons Startups Fail*. New York: CB Insights. Running out of cash is far more common as a reason for failure than having the wrong team, the wrong marketing or charging too much.
5. Christensen, C. and Overdorf, M. 2000. Meeting the challenge of disruptive change, *Harvard Business Review* (March–April).
6. Pychyl, T. 2009. Fear of failure, *Psychology Today*, 13 February.

Part Two

Connect

Chapter 6

Begin at the End

BEGIN AT THE END

Connect your vision to how you behave as a team *by describing success in 360 degrees*

Prepare for success

CONNECT

Everyone creates change

Sustain momentum

To build a vision of success, the best place to start is at the end.

In the previous section, we discussed the commitment of some wonderful groups of talented people at companies like Porsche and Fairline, who had extraordinary potential. But, as in many cases, the businesses had lost sight of where they were going, or why. At BMW, a successful business was missing the opportunity to create something remarkable because everyone, through no fault of their own, was focusing only on doing the next thing as well as they could.

In the first part of the book we looked at how you, as an inspiring leader, can dream a future, and how you can show everyone that they can commit to the same future, and how their commitment is vital to making that dream a reality. We saw how people everywhere can do extraordinary things when they commit to these goals and overcome their fear of flying. In this chapter, we look in more detail at how you align that commitment to the right goal.

At the end, you will have a clear idea of how you and your team can interrogate the business until it confesses its strengths and weaknesses. The honesty in this process of evaluation allows you to discover what success could look like for you. It's a vital part of the planning process, which we will cover next, and it is also essential to connect your inspiration to a real-life goal. When you begin at the end, you connect the dream to reality, and the way you work to the way you make progress.

It is easy to lose your way

As a leader, inspiring commitment might use a shared dream to energize your team to work hard, work well, do amazing things every day – but end up in completely the wrong place. If you do that you are destroying value, because that commitment could have been used to do something else (or they could have been working for someone else who could have used their skill for a better purpose). When the business drives itself into a ditch at high speed, often we conclude that the commitment everyone made was a waste of time, that the dream itself was wrong or that perhaps we just weren't smart enough.

There's another possible conclusion: that, while the dream was a good one, the commitment was total and the team was amazing – it just didn't have the control and direction it needed. You got distracted along the way, and soon the distractions were the business.

When you get commitment from the team your job as an inspiring leader has only just begun. Before you make a detailed plan of how you will achieve your dream, you need to think in detail about what success is, and how it is different to what you're doing today. You do this to remove the noise and distractions that have such an impact on your working life. Doing extraordinary things isn't just about knowing where you are going – it's about what you decide not to do as a result.

When you begin at the end, and plan your way back to where you are today, that gives you a route to success that's a straight line. Which is usually the quickest route.

In 2011, I spoke at a conference in Ireland about the principles of inspiring leadership, and what it can achieve for businesses that have lost their way. Afterwards, one of the audience asked me if I actually did the things I encouraged other people to do. I said that was exactly what I did, all the time when I wasn't making speeches, and so he invited me to visit Cape Town to give some advice to a company that he was a shareholder in.

To outsiders, Traderoot Technologies (Pty) Ltd was remarkably successful. They were doing plenty of business and had two offices, having added a sales team in Johannesburg. It had been set up in Cape Town, South Africa in 1999 as an eCommerce and payment technology platform, with amazing technology, excellent developers and a dedicated management team. In reality, however, the business was struggling.

Many mid-sized businesses struggle because they settle for the 3% growth I warn about, and gradually lose the ambition and commitment that initially created their success. You couldn't say that Traderoot's management lacked ambition, or wasn't working hard. Today we think of eCommerce as Amazon or Alibaba, and payment technology as Apple Pay, but for more than a decade they had been trying to build a much bigger, incredibly ambitious picture: the whole of buying, selling, payment and reconciliation, done electronically and instantly.

Most of us are protected from having to know how eCommerce is done, but every transaction that you and everyone else in the world does, creates many – sometimes hundreds of – other transactions. When you go into a shop and buy something, and pay with a bank card, then the shop's accounting system is updated, and its stock is debited. There may be a loyalty programme, or you might need delivery. Or there could be a warranty that's activated.

You might need to have your identity or address verified, or have the purchase checked against an order that the shop received from your company. You might need to be notified of any accessories, or warnings.

Then there's the financial side: the shop contacts your bank, which releases funds to the shop's account, while debiting your account and updating its records with the name of the retailer so that you can see it on your bank statement. Maybe you're getting credit, in which case there's a credit check using an online database, which has been updated with all your borrowing and assets.

It's hard to imagine that, only 20 years ago, much of this was done manually, using phone calls, the postal service and trust. Much of the information that was needed to do business was printed, posted and retyped into an incompatible computer system, leading to what are known as "fat finger" errors.[1] Stocktaking was done by going into a warehouse and counting. Filing cabinets were stuffed full of receipts and purchase orders (although, at the time, one analyst calculated that for every 20 pieces of paper filed, one would be lost for ever).

But, in 1999, it was the dream of Traderoot's founders to automate all of this, a dream that had been incredibly difficult for tech giants like IBM, Oracle and SAP to realize. They had built businesses creating large, complex IT systems for large, equally complex customers, but with limited success. The analyst firm Gartner has found that between 55% and 75% of all these projects, which often cost millions and take years, fail.

All of these technology providers had produced giant, cumbersome systems which were too expensive, too hard to configure and too difficult to use for most companies in the world. By 1999, the advantage of technology built on top of the internet was that it offered an innovative company like Traderoot a way to create entirely new, inexpensive ways to automate transactions.

The problem of short-term thinking

Traderoot had been created by smart people, and they built a very smart series of technology platforms. They were more flexible, more advanced and much cheaper than the big suppliers they competed against. At the beginning, success came easily.

Eugene von Engelhardt, the CEO Traderoot remembers:

"We started in 1999 with aspirations for global dominance. At that time, everyone was talking about what the internet could do for payment systems, and a subsidiary of Visa called Visa Internet Payment Gateway Systems (IPGS) wanted to create a way for people to pay on the internet, and they asked six companies to provide a proof of concept. We were the first to deliver, and show we could deliver transactions to Visa. We opened a US office, and were valued in 2000 at $100 million, though with no product yet, and no customers. But what you don't understand as naive entrepreneurs is business politics."

Soon afterwards, an internal reorganization at Visa abolished Visa IPGS, and with it Traderoot Technologies' $100m valuation. "In nine months, our whole future evaporated in front of our eyes. We went from 'the world is my oyster' to 'how do we keep the doors open?'" Eugene remembers. "Our executives spent a year and a half with no salary. Once I had to say to all our staff, there will be no salary for you this month. We were fighting every day for survival."

Traderoot's eCommerce platform continued to outshine the competition. It achieved 10 world firsts, and in 2011 it was the first platform to use MasterCard's pre-authorized, prepaid debit product, PayPass. By the time I met them, they were doing business with some of Africa's largest and most successful businesses, saving them millions of rand and helping them innovate, all with a company of about 30 staff. The founders had dreamed, and that part of the dream had come true.

But, at the same time, Traderoot's innovators accidentally did what many entrepreneurs do: they lost sight of how to commercialize this wonderful product. They knew the amazing things they could do, but they didn't know exactly what they should prioritize, where they were headed or, most important as it turned out, what they should not be doing. They had set up a sales and marketing organization called Traderoot Africa to keep cash coming in. It was selling to large, demanding customers and the price of success was that they were being pulled this way and that by every demand that those customers had, while at the same time they were cutting prices to win contracts.

"There was also a culture shift among our shareholders and board," Eugene says. "Much of our planning was centred on Traderoot Africa, because it was generating revenues, and we forgot that we had a global business to build through Traderoot Technologies. It became very difficult in the boardroom, because we had limited resources and both Traderoot Africa and Traderoot Technologies were competing for it."

There was also the distraction of the FIFA World Cup 2010 in South Africa. Traderoot built a ticketing and eCommerce platform which could deliver vouchers on every ticket for food and drink provided by FIFA partners. When customers used the vouchers, it would deliver information about who, where and when they were used to those brands. It was wonderful technology, but Traderoot didn't win the contract. Nevertheless, shareholders and board had tasted the excitement of the entertainment and hospitality business. It was now, effectively, three businesses, none of which had a coherent vision.

Traderoot had lost sight of what it had set out to do, because some members of the team were obsessed with winning business at almost any cost. It had fallen victim to the "winner's curse" – when companies compete for business, the winner often offers to do the most, at the cheapest price, and so a company like Traderoot wins mostly unprofitable business.

On my first day visiting Traderoot, I walked into reception at the same time as another visitor.

In reception, he said, "Do you work here?"

I said, "No, I've just come to do some consultancy for them."

"Good luck with that," he said, knowingly.

So I asked him where exactly he was visiting from, and he told me he was from SARS. Which, on my first visit to South Africa, didn't mean much to me until he explained: he was from the South African Revenue Service, and he had come to collect his overdue tax bill by seizing Traderoot's assets.

While I discussed strategy with the directors on the first morning, our visitor was wandering around the offices measuring the furniture, writing on his clipboard the value of everything he found. While the developers were working minor miracles for Traderoot's business clients, helping them to control their finances and achieve sustainable success, the South African Revenue Service was deciding how much it could make by taking the developers' desks away. When the directors eventually got home at night, they were holding garage sales to raise cash to put into the business.

Traderoot is an extreme example, but thousands of businesses fail every year for the same reason. According to Bloomberg, 8 out of 10 entrepreneurs go bankrupt in their first year, for a variety of reasons, most of which can be grouped under the heading: "Forgetting why you are here in the first place". Note that Traderoot had dared to dream. It was brave, and had taken a leap into the unknown. Everyone in the Cape Town office worked together. Ironically, if everyone had been less committed to the team, it perhaps wouldn't have been in the trouble it was.

Interrogating the business

It wasn't hard, I discovered, to find out how this had happened. The talent and dedication of the developers was being used to build anything and everything that Traderoot Africa, based 1,400km away in Johannesburg, demanded. The sales team's question to prospects was "what would you like us to build?" and when the prospects asked for something, their answer was always "yes".

When I asked: "Explain to me what we sell, to whom, and for what purpose?" the answers were confusing, and sometimes contradicted each other.

Traderoot had one company, two offices and at least two versions of the truth. The Cape Town business was losing money, but the Johannesburg sales organization thought it was *making* a lot of money, because all the costs were in Cape Town and all the revenues came through Johannesburg. Cape Town was developing the product. Johannesburg was selling the product, but it wasn't paying for the product. It was a mess.

The developers in Cape Town were custom-building products for clients with more and more functionality, not because they wanted to, but because the sales team had previously promised the clients that this is what they would provide, at unsustainable costs, to win business. Often with complex IT projects, the client doesn't know what it wants. They want their problem to go away, but they don't know how to do it.

After a year of talking to Traderoot, being impressed by their dedication and talent, but wary of their "strategy", I signed on as the chairman. We built an emergency 100-day plan with the team to stabilize the company and make sure that the tax office wouldn't take the computers away, while a finance director colleague that I had asked to help and I interrogated the business, to see what it would confess.

The interrogation is one of the most positive things you can do, but that doesn't mean it is quick or easy to ask people to think in this way when they have been living through a crisis. In this process, we are trying to identify the fundamental strengths of the business, and to recognize the assets we can learn as a new vision of success. Not everyone is going to come out of the interrogation happy. I did not want the Traderoot team just to say, "we have to do it like this" and then go back to thinking how much it would have to give away to sign the next deal.

The interrogation, and the plan that came out of it, was a process of helping everyone remember why they got into the business before they lost their way. To do this, I ask companies like Traderoot to think about success not just as an abstract idea, but to picture it in 360 degrees.

Success in 360 degrees

Don't rush this. I normally end up in a room after a couple of days with flip-charts and paper stuck all over the walls. Just because it takes a long time isn't an excuse to indulge in backward-looking thinking.

No more war stories Everyone knows that's how it used to be, but the only useful lesson is that the past is often a bad model for the future.

Money and status don't matter right now We know that investors and owners have put a pile of money in, but at that precise moment their money is worth zero. This is the sunk cost fallacy – that we have invested so much that we must keep going, working harder at the same, failing thing. All that matters is what you can do in the future, the chance of success and the rewards if you succeed, not the amount that you have already committed to the pot.[2]

Not everyone will commit, so create a path out of the business When we interrogate the business, we are also getting to know and understand the team. You are the leader, but you are not a dictator. Not everyone will follow you and, if that's their choice, it is better you don't try to cling on to them so they can confuse the clarity of the message. Defining where you are going means you might have to look around the table and work out who is going to be with you on this journey and who isn't, and take some hard decisions. Let the managers manage, and let the leaders lead, and anyone who wants to go in a different direction has to get out of the way. Because, otherwise, it will become a mess.[3]

When we thought carefully about it, the mission statement we came up with was "To be the de facto standard in e-commerce platforms and technology globally by maintaining an innovative culture". On the one hand it's a big dream, but on the other hand it's a much more focused dream than Traderoot's sales team were offering in 2011 which, as Eugene recalls, was a strategy of "trying to be everything to everybody". In creating a coherent statement of purpose, we immediately decided many of the things that we didn't want to be (an entertainment and ticketing company would be one high on everyone's list).

For a long time, those things seemed to have been building the future, but they were distracting the team from its goal. Eugene remembers it like this:

"We needed to take out the internal noise and remind the business what it once was.

We needed to believe in the same thing, be accountable in the same mechanism, and do our different jobs based on the same plan, so we could commercialise our effort. We knew it was critical if we are going to build a dependable team culture, and it would also show us that we didn't need to chase after every opportunity."

But many businesses have mission statements, and most of them aren't worth the time you spend trying to work out what they mean. This is why I prefer to think about it in 360 degrees:

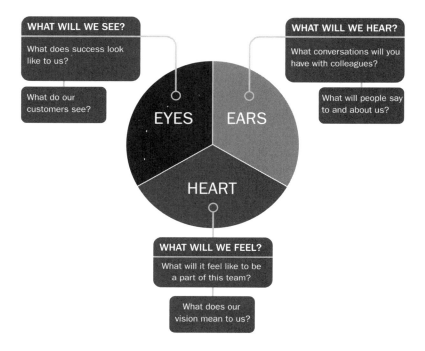

I want to know what I would be able to see, hear and feel if this dream was reality. It's a useful device, because every day afterwards it stops us wasting time by looking for goals that aren't part of this picture. This isn't about budgets or trade-offs at this point, it's a simple statement of what we want to be at our best. So, in Traderoot's case:

What will I see? If you imagine success, what do we see around us that wasn't there before?

Every major blue chip customer uses our standard platform to do business, and every bank uses our standard platform for reconciliation.

What will I hear? There are many ways to define this. What will people say about you when you're not in the room? What will customers say to you, and what will you say to them? How will you speak to each other? What conversation do you imagine having with a prospect?

If you want a bulletproof eCommerce platform that does your payment, your reconciliations, your international clearing, go to Traderoot.

You can prove that you're doing the right thing with data. eCommerce is not just about payments. It's about your whole environment.

We are creative and constructive. Our customers speak to us when they want help to build their future.

Instead of running a loyalty programme or a promotion, and then measuring the results at the end of the month, use our tool and you can watch it and tweak what's happening in real time.

What will I feel? But this is also an emotional commitment. Many companies are successful financially, but look at the faces of the employees as they arrive for work. This is not some wishy-washy promise to make everyone feel valued. The 360-degree view is about the emotion that drives us to keep going.

We will feel an enormous sense of pride in what we've built. We'll feel enormous enthusiasm for how we are transforming parts of the world, and transforming people's lives.

This process has several important outcomes:

One Version of the Truth (OVT) It is tempting to tolerate groups who want to define their own path. Using initiative is a good thing if it contributes to the overall goal (later we will discuss why it's pointless, and ultimately impossible, to micromanage an inspired team – so you positively need independent thinking). But there also has to be OVT. One day I was visiting the sales office, and found that they were looking for a better office space. They were, they assured me, struggling for space.

At this point you could have played football in between their desks, but even that was not the point.

"Do you not understand," I said, "that the group of which you are a subsidiary is about to fail?"

They did. But that wasn't part of their vision of success or failure. They had a different definition of success, which was having a more prestigious office. This was about as far off the straight line to realizing our dream as it was possible to get. Defining success in 360 degrees is defining common goals and ensuring everyone commits to the same vision.

Rebuild trust For Traderoot, this deceptively simple process meant the guiding principle of the business was a revolution in how they would behave. At a basic level, they would no longer try to win a contract by pitching for it at an unsustainable price. They could support the management in a positive way. When things are going badly, we often look for someone to blame, and sometimes we settle on the most visible person. At Traderoot, many of the executives who were taking the criticism had actually been holding the business together. So it was a case of trusting them and supporting them to re-inspire the team.

Remembering why we got out of bed today We remembered that Traderoot's mission was genuinely about transforming the world, and not just about helping retailers, consumers and banks to save money (though of course we could do all of that). Success would be tied to a bigger goal of making people's lives easier by transforming the way they shopped and did business.

We did focus on providing payment systems, reconciliation systems and loyalty systems to the major blue chip clients that are Traderoot's strength, clients that trust us and had often been dealing with Traderoot for years. We didn't promise to build platforms from scratch at unaffordable prices for people we didn't know.

Creating space to dream

Guess what? Simplifying Traderoot's mission was one of the most inspiring steps we could have taken. We found that the depth of this commitment was staggering – because in directing the thinking of talented people, they discovered a range of problems that fitted those targets.

For example, one of South Africa's largest chain of drug stores could use Traderoot's platform to get immediate feedback on its promotions, and take that back to its suppliers to achieve better discounts.

Or, Traderoot could start to talk and think constructively about how it mapped its mission to special groups of customers. In South Africa, there are millions of people on low incomes who have no formal relationship with a bank. One of the major regional financial services companies has been using the Traderoot platform to do business with them because, by automating transactions through a mobile phone, the cost is much lower. Now others are using the same platform to offer services through the post office, where non-traditional customers are more comfortable.

In *Built to Last*, the book in which Jim Collins and Jerry Porras track 18 successful companies, they discovered that 14 of the 18 had what they called a "Big Hairy Audacious Goal", or BHAG.[4] Collins wrote that it was "like the moon mission . . . clear and compelling and a unifying focal point of effort – often creating immense team spirit . . . A BHAG engages people – it reaches out and grabs them in the gut. It is tangible, energizing, highly focused. People 'get it' right away; it takes little or no explanation."

He contrasts the mission statement of GE:

Become #1 or #2 in every market we serve and revolutionize this company to have the speed and agility of a small enterprise.

With a confusing one from Westinghouse:

Total Quality

Market Leadership

Technology Driven

Global

Focused Growth

Diversified

The difference is that Westinghouse's mission statement doesn't inspire action. It's impossible to read it and know how you can contribute to it.

Starting at the end has a similar role, but I think it is important to focus on the process as well as the outcome. The businesses in *Built to Last*, like GE, are so large that creating the BHAG isn't a process in which many people can participate. As an inspiring leader, your job is to guide and help your team create this insight for themselves. If they do it well, they can relate everything they see, say and feel at work to the process of achieving this goal.

At Traderoot, we have moved a long way toward this vision of success. You only have to walk into the office to see the changes. When I visited I always got what we called the cardboard chair, because it was so broken that I put cardboard on it. Our financial problems were that bad. But now, we've got new office furniture, and the place looks like a successful business, it sounds like a successful business, and people feel like they are in a successful business again. I see the same people who were working their way to a heart attack smiling and laughing. There is a plan on the wall.

There was some cost. Some staff walked away from the business, and we decided to walk away from two or three customers that we couldn't afford to keep. Recently I had to give the news to the chief executive of one of them. He was trying to insist that we built his payment system at a price we couldn't afford. We said no.

"I'll use someone else," he threatened.

But now, with a sense of clear direction to guide me, I was able to say: "Of course, that's your choice."

Even Traderoot's motto is about the end, not the beginning – it is: "perfecting commerce". The previously closed Johannesburg office is open again, and the team now has 50 people. In 2016 sales grew 30% (not, you note, 3%). As I write, we are on plan to grow 60% next year, and 60% the year after, though nothing is certain. Traderoot won strategic e-Commerce business of the year for South Africa, and is now highly profitable. We completed one 1,000-day business plan, and are more than halfway through the second one. Traderoot doesn't owe any back taxes, so I won't bump into the guy from SARS in reception again.

But for the overwhelming majority of team members and customers, it has been a change for the better. "The first year of the plan caused a massive fallout with some people who did not want to come along for the journey. But we started to hear from customers that they liked the new model. They could see where we were going, and our plan made sense to them," Eugene says. Thinking clearly about its purpose in 360 degrees helped everyone at Traderoot share a clear vision of where it was heading.

Beginning at the end is an act of imagination. It makes the commitment you have demanded meaningful. It means, as a leader, that when you ask your team to commit, you can tell them what they are committing to achieve, and why. This gives direction to every meeting, conversation, project and email. The next step is to plan how you will get there.

Notes

1. These are errors caused by the need to retype numbers into a trading platform, rather than just trading electronically. For example, in May 2001 a dealer at Lehman Brothers was meant to sell £3 million of stock, and accidentally sold £300 million instead. The FTSE index plunged by £30 billion. Lehman was fined £20,000.
2. Thaler, R. 1999. Mental accounting matters, *Journal of Behavioral Decision Making*. 12(3): 183–206.
3. In one office, I found a culture that was so dysfunctional that one day I had to say to the guy in charge: "I can't tell if you are incompetent, or you're sabotaging the business." I told him that, despite explicit instructions to the contrary, he had just agreed to do a project for a client for a price that we couldn't possibly do, to implement a product that we didn't even have. He resigned. I didn't try to talk him out of it.
4. Collins, J. and Porras, J. 1994. *Built to Last*. New York: HarperBusiness.

Chapter 7

A Simple Plan

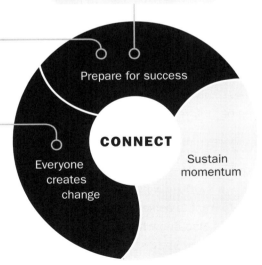

BEGIN AT THE END

Connect your vision to how you behave as a team *by describing success in 360 degrees*

A SIMPLE PLAN

Focus on the projects and priorities that make your vision real *by creating your 1,000-day plan*

Prepare for success

CONNECT

Everyone creates change

Sustain momentum

t's vital to make every day count. I have done this, over the years, by counting every day.

So far, we have concentrated on finding a dream, and making that dream into a vision, and creating a way that your team can understand and contribute to it. But you don't have as long as you think to make your vision become reality, and you can't inspire the people who work with you unless they know where you're taking them. Unless you methodically break down that process into manageable, achievable tasks, it will remain forever out of reach, and you will always look back on your dream as the thing you would have liked to have done, before you lost your way and settled for 3%.

In this chapter I will take you through the planning process I use with all the companies I work with, which produces what I call the "1,000-day plan", and how you show the people who work for you the value and meaning of their responsibilities to make the plan a success.

At the end of this chapter, you should be able to have a go at writing your own plan. It doesn't have to be for your business or department – I write a 1,000-day plan for myself, so that I make sure every day counts for what I want to achieve (writing this book was one of things on it). Hopefully, you will also know how to avoid some of the pitfalls of planning as I have seen it done in most businesses.

From planning to fail to planning to succeed

I often find that, when I say to executives that I'm working with, "Show me your business plan", they tell me it's in a cupboard. So we go to the cupboard, to fish the plan off a shelf and blow the dust off it. Often, they pull out a giant ring binder, full of detailed plans for the future that haven't come true.

I say: "When did you last read it?"

"Read it?" they say, looking confused, as if I'd missed the point.

Plans do not live in cupboards or on shelves. They live at the heart of the business. They live in the minds of everyone on your team, every day they are at work. No business is too large or small, successful or smart, to function without a plan, and every person inside that business should know how they are expected to contribute to making the plan work, and why. If you think that your planning holds you back, you're doing it wrong. It's the process that you've used to write it that's at fault. If your plan is hard to understand, or if it's as long as a book, or if no one knows what the plan is, or if they know what it is but don't understand what you're asking them to do, it probably does least damage if you stick it in the cupboard, or better yet, throw it in the bin. Then you are free to start again and do it properly.

As an inspiring leader, my job (and now your job) is to create this plan, which in turn creates the culture and the framework in which people can then exercise their natural genius. When they can do this, they are inspired to be the best they can be, and they take that plan and create something extraordinary from it. It's not complicated, it's creative, and it is fun to do. In later chapters, we're looking in more detail at what it means to be "better", what we mean by genius and how you avoid micromanaging that genius out of existence.

To do this, you don't need to do a course or spend more than a few pounds on flip-charts and a room. You will, however, need shared commitment, the discipline to tell one truth and follow the process no matter where it takes you, and the willingness to listen to good ideas and honest feedback – wherever they come from.

Planning is often seen as boring bureaucracy. Nothing could be further from the truth. The 1,000-day plans that I have used for more than 20 years have been the source of remarkable transformations. They saved careers, helped companies to achieve extraordinary results, made it possible for teams to transform the expectations of their customers and of each other, and moved small startups and big companies from the verge of bankruptcy into healthy profit.

Sir John Harvey-Jones ran the giant chemical company ICI during the 1980s. At that time, it was the largest company in the UK. He was, by any standards, an inspiring leader. In his first 30 months in charge of the company, he cut the UK workforce by one third, doubled the price of ICI shares and turned a loss into a profit of £1 billion, by meticulous planning. "Planning is an unnatural process," he said later, "it is much more fun to do something. The nicest thing about not planning is that failure comes as a complete surprise, rather than being preceded by a period of worry and depression."

The tendency to "do something" or a fear of the burden of red tape aren't the only distractions from planning that I frequently observe. To many it can feel like a distraction, or irrelevant. At Traderoot, recall that Eugene von Engelhardt's team established a 360-degree view of success, but planning did not come naturally. "It's not easy to plan for three years when we are thinking, I need to go out now and get the money to pay this creditor this afternoon," he remembers, "and as a software company we never planned on a daily basis because, in software, the sales cycle can last nine months. When you are building software, you can't always see daily progress."

Yet the change in attitude that business planning creates makes these problems less relevant because it changes the entire way the business is organized – everyone can understand how they are working in pursuit of a bigger dream. It is a way for everyone to monitor daily progress in the things that help to achieve a shared vision of success, without distraction.

You do not impose a plan. The plan, and the team following the process that sits behind it, will create it for you. What is even more surprising to people, when I show them the process for the first time, is that we can write this plan on *a single sheet of paper.* If you end up with a plan and you can't fit it on one sheet of paper, follow the process again, and plan better.

One of the advantages of having a single plan on a single sheet of paper is that everyone can look at it, every day. Put it everywhere, so that everyone knows they are on the same journey, no matter how tough it is. I often say to businesses when we make a plan, take some photographs, because in 6, 12 or 24 months you won't recognize this company. You will have bad days, and you will think you're not getting anywhere.

Then you can take out the pictures of how things were when you started out, look at them, and think: wow! Every day has counted after all.

You will live by this plan

If you ever get the opportunity to visit a Formula 1 motor racing team, you will discover to your surprise that their cars are not assembled from a warehouse of spare parts that are delivered from a factory. The team makes every piece of every car (except the engine, because that is built by the engine manufacturer). Every screw, nut and washer is created according to a plan, and is checked, tested and transported around the world.

There are approximately 80,000 of these components in each car. The engine revs up to 18,000 rpm, three times as fast as a road car's maximum, which means that the piston travels up and down 300 times a second. The carbon fibre brake discs have an operating temperature of 1,000°C. Each car has 100 sensors, and contains about 1km of cable.[1]

When you are building something like this, it's not hard to imagine that deviating from the plan isn't just a matter of success or failure, profit or loss, it can be a matter of life and death. If you're 99.9% accurate, that's 80 parts that haven't been installed properly.

But this is the sort of attention to detail that your business needs to have if it's going to be successful. Every business, no matter how small, consists of thousands of separate actions that all have to be done correctly. When you are moving at full speed that is not the time to try to change or fix the plan, just as a Formula 1 engineer can't mend the car when it is moving at 300km/h.

As an inspiring leader, you cannot hope to be in charge of every tiny detail that makes your team safe, professional and profitable. You cannot speak to every customer or check every product, because you will never have the time – and, more importantly, because you have another job already. So you need a process by which the individual workers, or the team members, make their own decisions at the point of contact with the real world, and which gives everyone the confidence that everyone will, to the best of their ability, do the right thing.

That's why the plan is the fundamental element of inspired leadership. Without the attention to detail of the engineers in creating a car that is as fast as possible, a Formula 1 team is useless. Without the contribution of everyone to your plan, your dream will remain a fantasy.

Therefore, you need to create a culture so that everybody else uses their eyes, their knowledge, their intelligence and the 5% inherent genius that we all have to make sure that attention to detail is part of the entire organization. The only way you can achieve that alignment is by ensuring everybody knows and agrees with where we're going. You might not be building one of the world's fastest cars, but you want to be world class at what you do, and that means taking it seriously. A member of an inspired team never walks past a piece of litter, never misses a deadline unless there's a good reason (and that reason has a higher priority in the planning that you have done), and never gives up on the dream – and nor should you. If a bin is full, you empty it. If your desk is a mess, you tidy it.

Planning will help you to do this, because when you are part of a process, these small actions have meaning and purpose. A plan creates a way of working that everyone understands, and which means that everyone's work gets you closer to your vision of success.

In the previous chapter I described how Traderoot changed its vision of success by painting a picture of it in 360 degrees: how success looks, how it sounds, how it feels. This is stage zero of the planning process. You can't plan unless you know what you are planning to do, but it doesn't tell you what your team will do next, tomorrow or next month.

I'm going to describe the planning process in a lot of detail. There are two reasons for this. First, the detail of the process is important if you want to get a useful result. There are far more people who tell you to make a plan than have actually done it successfully, and the methods I use have worked time and time again. Like the team that creates a Formula 1 car, every element of the plan has to be created, examined and tested until it is right, and you need to lead that process. The second is that consistency is just as important as the ability to dream. No one creates the world's best plan by cutting corners, skipping the boring bits or thinking, "how hard can it be?" Trust the process, and follow it with intent.

This is not, however, just your process, and the plan does not belong to you. You inspire your team to create it for themselves, so it belongs to them. Your contribution is a gift to them, and they share it equally, because they had a hand in creating it.

When our teams go away for a couple of days to start our planning, I prefer to take people from every level and department of the business. If you're a small startup, everyone can take part. At Fairline, 20 people did our strategic planning, including boat-builders and executives. Even at BMW, 30 of us went offsite to take part in planning. It you decide instead that a few executives and consultants will go to a hotel, write a plan, come back and say to their team, "now do that", it's much less likely to work in my experience – simply because the plan belongs to management, not to the business. It's hard to commit to someone else's dream, especially if you have no idea why those priorities were chosen.

Creating ideas

Usually, if I'm leading the planning process, I will show the others what our planning process has achieved in the past. This is the untapped potential in every company, the opportunity that will not escape us this time. They know that there is opportunity because every time they are frustrated at work as a result of something that should be done and isn't, they are imagining a better version of the company. Now, I say, let's build that together.

For two days, when we're in this room working as a team to fix the business, we're all equal, because this is about the capacity to have good ideas. Everyone's ideas are equal, and everyone will bring different dimensions to the process because everyone is doing different things. If you take a large team, it is your responsibility to make it work – make sure that everyone works together, everyone contributes and cliques don't form. Perhaps some of the people you have in the room aren't used to being asked for ideas, or aren't used to having their opinions listened to.

But, while everyone's ideas carry weight, you are still leading this process, and you are still tasked with making sure the plan works at a later date. So remember: if something gets out of control, your team will look to you to be the disciplinarian, to control the meeting and make sure that everyone feels they can contribute.

Discover the 360-degree view of success

Remember from the previous chapter, you need to know that your vision for the business is authentic. What does it look like? What does it sound like? What does it feel like? This vision will guide everything you do afterwards, so it must be right.

You will also have principles. How do you do work? What is important not to compromise on?

Identify what you need to do to be better

To get there, what are the challenges you face? Where do we need to improve, and what should we be focusing on to achieve that vision of success? You don't need to differentiate between the things that you're not doing now that need to be done, or improving the things that you do. But honesty about where the business needs to be better is the foundation of making the dream work.

Once the ideas start coming, make sure they are grouped on flip-charts into different subject headings. As long as those headings mean something coherent for the business, it doesn't matter exactly what they are, and they shouldn't be your traditional silos – you might want to reorganize the business to make the plan work better. Typically, that might mean people, process, client needs, IT. Put them around the wall, and break the teams into smaller groups.

How do you solve your problems?

Their next task is to describe what a world-class way to solve that problem would look, sound and feel like.

All that matters is that you are not scared to face the challenge of dreaming. It's not about finding the solutions at this point, or allocating budgets, or thinking about how you did it last week, it's about setting goals. Your job here is to make sure the team sticks with the process, and doesn't start telling war stories or closing down ideas because they're not practical. You want to be able to think about ideas that are impractical: some of the best ideas start as bad ideas that make you think.

It is tempting to drift from the goal that you want to have absolutely the best way of handling customer complaints in the industry to writing down "Install CRM software". This is what average businesses tend to do. Don't slip back into 3% thinking, because installing software isn't part of your vision. No one has a dream that they get a new application on their desktop on Monday, and your customers don't care what your software is. They do care about the experience they receive though. At this point (although not for ever), it doesn't matter how you're going to achieve it, or how much you paid for it last year. It is *what* you dream of achieving – absolutely the best handling of customer complaints – that you need to capture, and that is based on the vision you created: what will your customers see, say and feel?

What matters is that you have captured the idea of being *as good as it is possible to be* – in my companies we use the term "world class" to describe it – that you have been honest about where you fall short, and that you're not duplicating ideas. Collect every idea. Write them on sticky notes. Capture everything, don't talk about budgets. Open your mind and imagine instead. You can put anything you like on that wall.

Create key strategic areas (KSAs)

Now you can start to aggregate those sticky notes into groups. One group might be called "business development", one might be called "financial". Don't force them into pre-conceived categories on a spreadsheet, or job functions, or existing departments. Look at what's on the board, and let the categories emerge. What you need to do in the future isn't necessarily guided by what you did until this moment.

I often find that, before long, some of the headings that you grouped your ideas under merge into each other, because the vision that would solve one of the challenges also solves others, or because they represent the old way of doing things that suddenly seems less relevant. So the problems in product and marketing, or your research and technology, or finance and HR may merge, because they have a common cause. And what you are left with are a small number of key strategic areas – part of the business – which are the focus of the 1,000-day plan. The teams I work with tend to identify five or six, though your number might vary. (This rule-of-five is not surprising. If you have 8 or 10 KSAs the plan will be hard to manage, with too many goals for teams to aim for, and there is probably overlap between some of the KSAs. If you have one or two KSAs, that's a short-term stabilization plan, not something that will drive the business for 1,000 days without being completely reworked.)

Group those key priorities (KPs)

This is an exciting, daunting and slightly chaotic moment. In the room, you have five or six sheets of flip-chart paper with headings on, and 50 yellow notes of ideas for change stuck to each one. Those yellow notes are now the key priorities for the business: the tasks that the team has suggested to make your performance in each KSA world class.

What typically comes up that's unexpected is, actually, the solutions are a lot simpler than most people thought. Get the product right, get the price right, get the communication right, make sure that customer service is what the customers would imagine is world class. It sounds simple, but helping a team discover it for themselves can amaze everyone in the room. However, the list of things that you have decided to do will be as long as that wall.

Prioritize, prioritize, prioritize

At this point, we introduce the game that I call prioritize, prioritize, prioritize. The game has three rounds, but the others in the room don't know that yet.

Prioritize

The first task for the team will be to take those lists of KPs in each key strategic area, and rank them in order of priority. Make sure they know that this isn't sentimental, and isn't about their pet projects, and what would be nice to have or easiest to do. To be world class in your KSAs, what do you need to do first? What's most important? Challenge the team to be practical.

This might cause some debate. After all, it's not comfortable for anyone, including the team leader, to see our favourite ideas, plans or projects demoted. At a time like this, when we dare to dream about a different idea of success, then we can realize that we have become emotionally attached to zombie projects that aren't going anywhere (and probably wouldn't make much difference to anyone if they succeeded). Often, they live on because we thought of them, or the status of some team members is attached to them.

There are times in my experience when we need to have these tough debates in which everything is up for grabs. They can be difficult, but it is vital that priorities are discussed thoroughly and openly at this stage. Something has to be the most important, and something has to be least important.

While harmony is important, there's sometimes good reason to encourage honest debate. Mathias Dewatripont and Jean Tirole, two economists who specialize in the way that businesses are organized, have analysed this problem and concluded that businesses that encourage their people to sometimes argue openly for their point of view are healthy. One of the most important benefits is that this debate, provided it is resolved amicably, and has a finishing point, helps deepen the team's commitment to the outcome – even from members of the team who didn't agree with the idea at the outset. When there's a healthy debate, the chance that people will "go with the flow", without committing to make the idea happen or support it internally, reduces. Ultimately, even if some people don't get their way all the time, listening to the arguments can help teams to get behind a plan.

Making people prioritize in this way flushes out the tired arguments of "that's the way we do it around here". It also forces people to think about how they could spend their time most productively. We all have to prioritize at work, because there aren't enough hours in the day – but unless we think carefully about what is the best use of our time rather than focusing on the thing that is distracting us, or the email that catches our attention, we're not making the best plan.

If vigorous debate is a good thing, destructive conflict is not. The best teams promote debate, but debate that's constructive. Companies that are underperforming have these arguments every day. But without a process to find a positive outcome and use it, the debates happen behind the scenes, with no resolution, and no outcome in a change of priority or even a broader look at why they are doing what they do. This is often dismissed as just office politics. If we are honest, it is simply a waste of energy, and it damages the business. The negative energy feeds the energy vampires, the people who take care to explain why everything that the team does is wrong, how every achievement is meaningless and how every plan will probably fail anyway.

So when I do this exercise, I am sure to explain this early, and clearly:

When you agree to this plan, this is what we're going to do. When we walk out of this room, we all support it 100%. Because, if you don't, you will undermine our team.

At the end of the prioritization process, there's a simple representation of the priorities: the notes that people have placed at the top of the list are the most important. Ask everyone to have a walk around, make sure they are all comfortable with that prioritization. They will not be allowed to change their minds when they get back in the real world, and have to put the plan into operation. This is a moment to commit.

Sometimes passionate arguments break out about whether something should be priority 21 or 22. Which is fine. They don't know what's coming next. When everyone is comfortable, when they have walked around the room and not found anything to disagree with, it's time for round two.

Prioritize, prioritize

At this point, there's a new task. Ask each team to count halfway down the list. Everything below that they must take off the wall, and store the Post-it notes in a box. I call the box the birdcage, which I will explain.

The first reaction you will hear from the team: but we need to do these things! That is why you need to take them off the board, and out of consideration for now. We have 1,000 days to get through this plan. Your team has created literally hundreds of projects to complete. It's simply not possible to do them all, so even the best work would seem like failure.

Because everyone has actively agreed that the projects in the bottom half are less important, and because they had the chance to argue for any of them but did not take it, we can conclude that the projects that remain on the board are the half to pick. You might have 60–100 projects at this stage, which is daunting enough.

We don't throw away the ideas that didn't make the cut, we keep them, just in case we need them. I used to say put them in a box, but the leader of one of the startup businesses I work with showed me the value of naming things well when you're in a situation like this. Lindy Scott runs Conceptual Eyes, a young creative agency based in Johannesburg, South Africa. It specializes in internal communication. She approached me about 1,000 days ago for advice. She had a dream to build a different kind of creative agency – one that helps clients to become extraordinarily successful by focusing the investment made in their internal communication. Done well, internal communication can ensure that moments like this, when there will be a mixture of emotions, some resentment, and maybe the potential for misunderstanding, can have a huge impact on the company's growth and development.

Lindy taught me that words create images, images create emotions, emotions drive effort, effort drives progress. It's because they are valuable and precious ideas: they're just not ready to fly yet. We want the team to keep hatching the ideas which will fly when they are ready.

Internal communications is one of those skills that many leaders assume they have, or don't see as a priority. But, at times like this, being able clearly to explain what you are doing, why you are doing it and helping to show everyone why it has a benefit for them makes a big difference.

After this, take more time to reprioritize the ideas that remain. With half the ideas in the birdcage, some things that only just made the cut become more important, maybe because they're now the only project in that area. We all agree again on our priorities, and it's time for a break. That was difficult to do, and there's still round three to come.

Prioritize, prioritize, prioritize

It's time for the hardest cut of all. When we're back in the room, there is one final exercise: take the shortened list, count halfway down, and split it. We're not just going to focus on the top 50%. We're going to focus on the top 25%.

We don't put the ideas that didn't make the cut at this stage into the birdcage, because they are important. We split them, and put them below a line. They are important, but they're not part of the plan right now. We may return to them one day, but not for now. The team has to deliver with complete focus and commitment on the top 25%, which is usually between 30 and 50 projects, in the next 1,000 days. We need to implement the changes and consolidate them fully into the business so that they become a stable and effective part of our new way of operating. If we finish before 1,000 days (and sometimes that happens), then we can go to the second 25%. If we finish those, we can open the birdcage and let other projects fly. But the prioritization exercise, brutal as it is on the ideas that everyone has of the business, means that at the end of the 1,000 days there will not be 100 half-finished projects in a business that is broadly unchanged.

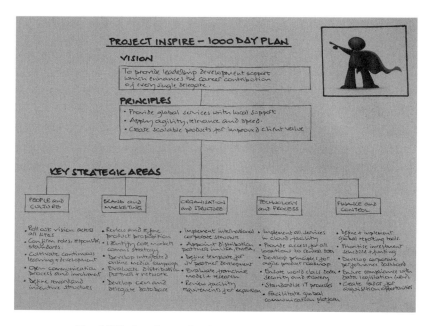

The 1000 day plan – simple, readable, focused, visible

Thirty projects, spread across five areas. That's what we're going to deliver. That's the 1,000-day plan. It looks like this (this is a real plan).

Writing the plan

As you can see, one of the important benefits of a plan made in this way is that it fits on one large sheet of paper, listing all the projects, who is accountable for them, and what we aim to achieve – in sum, this is every-thing we will set out to do in the next 1,000 days, or until something (the market, the business or our own success) causes us to review it. Typically, we hold a formal review of the plan and our progress against it every 200 days. This gives us a chance to adapt, adjust or confirm progress.

When these plans are written out, I encourage the team to hand-write them on a big sheet of paper. It would be quicker to draw them in PowerPoint, but a handwritten plan is more intimate. It is something that we crafted together, just as much as any other product the business builds or service it creates. This is a living, working tool, not another corporate poster or half-forgotten slide in the corporate deck.

And, of course, it has to have a name. As team leader, I have one rule for naming plans: call it what you like. The name your team chooses will tell you something about how they see this adventure. I have seen Project Phoenix (no surprises for guessing that was a turnaround), Project Condor (the highest-flying bird), Project Horizon (for success as far as we can see) and many more.

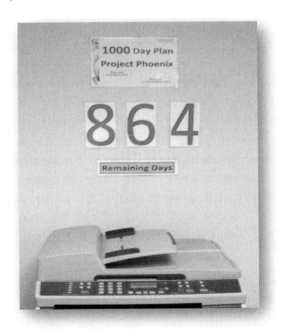

Raise the heart rate – count every single day

Another one of the companies I'm working with has named its 1,000-day plan "The 1,000-day plan" – and they are a creative agency! But every 200 days, they review and analyse their progress and determine the correct priorities for the next 200 days to ensure they reach their vision of success. For the next 200 days, they are running "Think Pink". The plan needs them to drive sustainable revenue generation. In the way they prepare their accounts, "pink" means profit to the team, and for the next 200 days they discipline their decision-making by remembering to "Think Pink".[2]

Then, it is time to communicate the plan to the business.

Communicating the plan

The way that a plan is presented is critical and needs careful thought. I have preferred not to introduce it with razzmatazz, but we do spend time and effort to introduce it properly. Not everyone in the team was involved in the planning process, and so we need to ensure that they understand what we did, and how we built the plan – but, more importantly, why we built the plan, and what success will look like.

I have always preferred to introduce the plan to groups in a relatively informal environment where they are free to ask questions, which means a maximum of 100 people at a time. In big teams, this can mean repeating the message many times to different groups. You will be glad you invested this time though. It is crucial to the success of the plan that everyone understands why it is on the wall, and accepts it.

There is more to a plan than 30 projects – no matter how important they may be – and a memorable name. Any 1,000-day plan has to have meaning to everyone in the business, at every level, on every one of those 1,000 days. You need to make every day count by giving every day meaning. In the picture above, day 864 has to have a purpose: it is the day on which something is scheduled to happen. Therefore, after this plan has been agreed, you need to get your hands dirty by planning everything you need to do to deliver your goals, in detail.

Too many business plans are a set of vague outcomes or long-term objectives. Remember, every leader is a dreamer, but not every dreamer is a leader. It is critical that the plan underpins the dream. It is key that the plan is visible, relevant and part of everyday activity. To avoid the problem that the plan gets forgotten we break the plan for each of the key priorities into manageable chunks. Some of the key priorities might be a 500-day project. This is 500 days for the complete project, taking into account everything that needs to be done to make it happen. But there is no point in creating a 500-day project and handing it over to your team. It will fail.

It fails because, if you say to the team, "in 500 days we're going to be at the top of that mountain", no matter how well they work or how committed they may be, by day 100, they've forgotten which mountain it was that they were meant to climb. So we break the 500-day project down to ten 50-day projects.

The 50-day project

By breaking every KP into manageable chunks, you make the plan meaningful, and you create a way to measure progress. When I plan these projects, each project has to have a five-day ramp up, to choose your team members, define the priorities for the next 50 days, reiterate the objectives and how we will measure success, and do all the briefing that needs to be done. Then there are 40 days of activity, as the team achieves its goals. Then a five-day handover, so while the business is ramping up the next project for that KP, the previous one is ramping down. That means consolidating and measuring what it achieved, capturing anything we've learned, and then moving on to the next 50-day phase.

By doing it in 50-day phases, you can celebrate at the end of those 50 days because something of value has been achieved. So your job, as an inspiring leader, can be to help people to appreciate that they are making progress, every 50 days. They have achieved something that makes the next stage possible, and they have contributed to the success of the team by doing it.

Teresa Amabile and Stephen Kramer are academics who have been researching how workers feel about their jobs for almost 20 years. Recently they asked 238 of them to keep a daily diary, and found that they would feel more motivated and committed if they could get regular small "wins" by breaking their work projects into smaller chunks. "When we think about progress, we often imagine how good it feels to achieve a long-term goal or experience a major breakthrough. These big wins are great – but they are relatively rare. The good news is that even small wins can boost inner work life tremendously," they say.[3]

Project management matters

Of course, with this many projects, and this many KPIs, and a permanent state of being in the beginning, middle or end of at least one strategic project, someone has to be the project manager whose job it is to monitor the plan, check we are on course and do something if the plan slips. It does not matter if you are leading a team in a three-person company or a three-million-person company, you must have a project manager, because somebody must be accountable. That person cannot be you, because you are busy leading the business or owning the company. Leaders and owners cannot give the detailed attention to following a plan that this job requires.

Note two things. This is now a process. We have committed to it. The project manager cannot rewrite the plan on a whim (or because someone wants to miss a deadline), and needs to be organized enough to realize when the process is not going well, and who to tell.

And the project manager has authority, even if he or she was not previously a senior figure in the hierarchy. This is not an administrative job, 1,000 days of ticking boxes. This is an important, high-profile role. Anyone trusted with the detail of managing hundreds of projects, with thousands of KPIs, must be trusted to speak truth to power, including board members or partners (who might sometimes decide that the process doesn't apply to them). You have all agreed that this process, if it is followed, is the best chance to create success, and so the project manager is the guardian of that commitment. Anyone who deviates from the process without a good reason might undermine the team if it's a serious enough distraction, and it is up to the project manager to observe that and, if necessary, to point it out.

Planning a culture of success

It's not just a question of making every day count: you also have to count every day. The first day, day 1,000, has to be an event. Everyone in the team has to know what day it is, every day.

Build a war room

We have our hand-drawn 1,000-day plan on the wall, and it looks rather friendly and informal, but behind it we have our professional project management process. I like the war room to have previously been something fancy – it sends a message. We convert the boardroom or the chief executive's meeting room, or some other nonsense. (I once sacrificed a private dining room that I had inherited when I took over to be the war room!) It says: there's nothing more important in this business.

The war room is open, anybody can go in there and read it. At Fairline, for example, where there was initially a huge gap between management and unions, I invited the union reps to have their meeting in the war room, because we all had a common interest in the success of the business, and I needed their help. They knew how to build boats, and I didn't.

They were understandably reluctant, but after we showed them around the war room they were our biggest advocates. They could see the changes we were making, because we mapped the progress on those walls.

The war room is the detail behind the 1000 day plan

Count every day

If you look back at the picture of Project Phoenix, it was day 864. The 1,000 day counters are as important as the plan. We start from day 1,000, 999, 998, . . . and this raises the heartrate of the business. People move faster. Instead of making decisions or taking action in weeks or months, we do it in days. People immediately start to think in days.

At Traderoot, this daily sense of purpose has been embedded in the office culture. Eugene explains how counting down has raised the heart-rate of the business:

"When we ran our business quarterly, it was not the best way to plan projects like ours because by the time you see a problem it is four or six months old. When you run the business daily, you see problems right away and can do something about them early. It means we were constantly ticking things off, constantly asking each other about progress, or reviewing what we had done. The shareholders and executive team see this progress too."

One Version of the Truth

Emphasize the principle of OVT by placing many copies of the plan in places where everyone who is part of the process can see them. This means that anyone can inspect it, because everyone deserves to know how well we are doing against the plan. The members of the team have bought into your dream. They have overcome their fear. They have committed to the process. They deserve truthful, open communication, whether the news is good or bad. Things go wrong in every plan, but communicating honestly, in my experience, gives you the best chance of fixing day-to-day glitches.

The planning process, with its emphasis on shared goals, helps to create OVT thinking. In turn, working to deliver that shared vision may also uncover communications gaps inside the team that can be filled. Eugene says:

"We put ourselves in a position in which we delivered a consistent answer, consistent services, and consistent products. Our customers knew that, when they do business with us, this is what we provide, this is what it does, and this is what it looks like. But when we were working this way, we realized we didn't have enough interdepartmental communication. For example, support didn't know about how we were working with the customer, so if they started getting calls, they didn't know how to help. We had to develop a customer-centric view, so support can say 'I can help you, let's get an engineer on the line' rather than 'you need to call another number'. The other thing we realized was that there was a lot of folklore. When we wanted to know how something worked, we had to get someone in the business to come and tell us. To improve accuracy and quality we had to get all our documentation and libraries into place too."

Don't sugar-coat

I don't make the news pretty as a way to encourage people, because the truth will catch up with us sooner or later. Part of your job as an inspiring leader is to get the team to recognize that those things are challenging. If they were easy to do, chances are you would have done them already. Also, the job of prioritizing what you have to do, rather than just what you want to do, means that many of the projects that some of the team may have deferred because they considered them "too hard" are now "priority one" in the plan. They may have got put to one side because they were gritty, a bit like hard work, and we're not quite sure where to start with them. But, those are the things that are going to transform the business. We all know it, and that is why we put them into the top 25%.

Make sure that you are not tempted to rebrand failure as success. The entire reason for this process is to deal with the real problem in the business. I recently watched a CEO present to his team. "We are winners," he told them, having shown them a chart with sales that had dropped for each of the last five years. He successfully cut costs during this time, so profits were up, but this was not a business of winners, and everyone in the room will have known that. They had not addressed the big issues in the business. They were not inspired.

But fear and threats are short-term motivators. So let's try to think differently about the hard stuff, too. Now, let's change our mindset so that we have fun doing those things. Let's make putting a new computer system in fun. How do we do it differently so it's fun? How do we do this in a different way than any company's ever done it before?

Avoid a meetings culture

To minimize the reporting, we have a sheet for each one of the 50-day projects that slides into a clear plastic wallet in the war room. It has to be updated every week with progress against the KPIs. We use a simple RAG status (Red – off track, Amber – getting there, some challenges, Green – on track) colour coding system. Anyone can walk around the war room and almost immediately see how well we are doing against target.

There's no written report, so there are very few words on this sheet. It defines the project and what we've achieved. Underneath, we place a more detailed report which tracks 10-day intervals, so we can see what's going on in detail. If that's all red, there's something wrong – you can find the manager and ask: "What's going on here?" But, if they are green, walk past them. You can manage in two minutes by walking around that room and seeing where the red spots are. Meanwhile, everyone else can get on with their jobs.

It's a plan, not a tablet of stone

A thousand days is a long time, especially for a turnaround or a startup technology business. As you change, so your aspirations might change. Your markets might change, or you might find that the plan isn't quite right.

Therefore, though everyone has agreed on the plan, it's not the end of the conversation. When I have meetings, I prefer to have them standing in front of our ideas wall (if you remember, that's the wall on which anyone can write a bright idea, at any time), discussing how we're going to achieve the aims and objectives that we've put in our 1,000-day plan. And this is where you're trying to capture the 5% genius in everyone on the team. We'll look more into how you capture genius in a later chapter.

It's not always obvious how best to accomplish the tasks in the plan. And the plan cannot become a prison. In both cases, the first people who have an idea are probably the ones who walk past the ideas wall every day as they do their jobs, and who maybe used to complain that "nobody ever asks me". Well, now you do. If the team comes up with an idea that should be on the list, put it on the list.

An example of something we got wrong: at Fairline, we were struggling to survive at first. We decided that designing a new boat wasn't a priority. Back in the real world, this hurt us in a way we hadn't predicted. Fairline, the press said, didn't have a product strategy. Therefore, it was legitimate to worry whether the company would be around in the long term, which meant that some potential customers weren't prepared to commit millions of pounds to commission us to build a new boat for them. What was clear was that we needed a proper strategy, and we needed a new product, and to make sure the market was aware of it, and that was a key priority.

So, we made it one. You can read the story of how we did it in Chapter 10.

We didn't have the money to build a physical boat, so we listened to a young, smart designer and designed and built a virtual boat that captured all our most innovative thinking, using computer graphics, in 50 days. When we showed it to the press, it captivated their attention. We were, they agreed, a brand with a clear vision of the future.

Planning has a bad reputation as dull, restricting micromanagement. It's hard work, but done properly it communicates the meaning of the commitment we have shared. It speeds up the heartbeat of the business, it doesn't slow it down.

Planning is a joint responsibility, led by you. But when you have written your plan your work has just begun. During the 1,000 days, your job will be to help create a higher quality team, with more ideas, that knows how to run itself. That's what we're going to have a look at next.

Notes

1. Valimaki, C. 2017. Formula 1 racing. *Chemical-materials.elsevier.com*.
2. In 2007, Marks and Spencer launched "Plan A", an inspiring environment-friendly plan made up of 100 commitments over five years, based on sourcing responsibly, reducing waste and increasing community work. Why Plan A? Because, in the words of Mike Barry, the company's head of sustainable business, "There is no plan B."
3. Amabile, T. and Kramer, S. 2017. *The Progress Principle: Using Small Wins to Ignite Joy, Engagement, and Creativity at Work*. Boston: Harvard Business Review Press.

Chapter 8

Don't Be a Genius,
Make a Genius

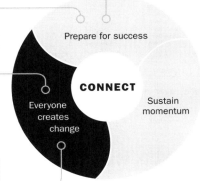

BEGIN AT THE END

Connect your vision to how you behave as a team *by describing success in 360 degrees*

A SIMPLE PLAN

Focus on the projects and priorities that make your vision real *by creating your 1,000-day plan*

Prepare for success

CONNECT

Everyone creates change

Sustain momentum

DON'T BE A GENIUS, MAKE A GENIUS

Uncover creativity that your team didn't know they had *by creating ways for bright ideas to flourish* very successful business I have been part of has succeeded not by outspending its competitors, but by outthinking them. To do this, you need smart ideas, that no one else has had, and those ideas need to come from the people around you.

The business plans that we discussed previously are only as good as the ideas that your team has to make them come to life. When you challenge your team to imagine how you could grow by 300%, your success directly depends on what they contribute. But many businesses draw a line between "creatives" and the rest of the business. There will always be insightful, original thinkers. But everyone has the potential to be a 5% genius. I want my 5% geniuses not to be afraid to have great ideas, and to be allowed to flourish.

In this chapter, we will look at how you, as an inspiring leader, can inspire creative genius and connect with all the bright ideas that teams often fail to capture until it is too late, if at all. Sometimes one good idea can change how your team sees its job, and how the rest of the world sees your business.

Your genius is waiting for you

Leadership is not about being a genius. It is about creating the culture for other people to contribute their genius to the team. Sometimes it's about recognizing that people have specific skills, and giving those people the freedom to apply those skills. The best example of this in my career was a statistical genius who I will call Jurgen, a person who worked for me in a team dominated by salespeople and managers, but who wasn't naturally either. He had, however, a knack for making sense of numbers.

In 2001, I joined a company called The EurotaxGlass's Group. This multi-syllable business had been created by the merger between two data-rich businesses, one from the UK (Glass's) and one from Switzerland (Eurotax), and was headquartered in Zurich, Switzerland.

For anyone who worked in the auto business in the UK, Glass's Guide was simply known as "the bible". It had been established in 1933, to capture the values of used cars. William Glass, who had created it, was more than 5% genius in his own right: among his creations were a machine gun that could shoot through the propellers of a military aeroplane, and an electric kettle that switched itself off when it boiled.

Long before the era of big data, Glass had realized the value of collecting sales statistics. He created a comprehensive record of car pricing to help both garage owners set a competitive sales price and consumers bargain for value when they wanted to buy and sell cars. As the first person to hold a car auction, he presumably also had an interest in using his own product.

In 1957, Hanns Schwacke had a similar idea, which he published first in Germany as the Schwacke Liste, and then across Europe under the brand name Eurotax. During the 1980s, both of these guides had produced electronic versions, and then online versions for the internet. By the turn of the century, the two databases contained inventories of the pricing of thousands of types of motor vehicle and their spare parts, in 28 countries.

Seeing the value of this, Hicks, Muse, Tate & Furst (HMTF), a Dallas-based private equity group, acquired Glass's Information Systems Ltd in 1998 and Eurotax AG in 2000, and merged them.

This was an exciting business from the outside. It had more than 600 staff, revenues of more than €120m, and at this time people were beginning to realize that data had huge potential to create rapid growth if it was used to create information.

But, like so many companies that had built a profitable business on doing things in one way, EurotaxGlass's struggled to innovate. Keron Hurlstone was an area sales manager at the time, working hard to sell the guide, on the road four days a week. She remembers:

"Glass's was very traditional. It was like a publishing house more than a company.

We recognized that online was the future, and tried to excite everyone to make that happen. I remember thinking that we were missing a trick, we were limited to the existing paper products that we could sell. We were committed to selling the book as a paper product, because that's where the advertising was at that time. But the book was not going to be around for ever, and the people who were very committed to not changing didn't understand that the advertising revenue was going to go down . . . there was a feeling in some parts of the company that 'we're Glass's guide, we don't do that'."

How could we unlock the value in the data, when many people in the business had little interest in radical change? Interrogating a business until it confesses its strengths also means looking for special skills in the team.

A senior manager in EurotaxGlass's at the time – I will call him Jurgen – was not an easy person to manage. He was incredibly bright but opinionated, demanding and argumentative. As a team, we took the Myers-Briggs personality test to establish our personality types and how we might work together more effectively. Jurgen was classified, among other things, as introverted and egotistical. We anonymized the tests to investigate how well we knew each other in the team. Everyone in the team identified

Jurgen immediately. Except, it turned out, Jurgen himself, who swore the reports must have been mixed up. If a large part of leadership is self-awareness, it is fair to say that he was not a born leader.

If he wasn't primarily a people person, Jurgen knew data. Now, in this newly merged group of companies, we had access to some very big data, which we had expected would provide value for the new generation of auto trade websites, as well as to our traditional dealerships. But, when we lifted the bonnet and peered at the engine of EurotaxGlass's data, we had a shock. All the country databases were independent, held on disparate platforms and structures, and with wildly different standards of data integrity. My CTO would describe it to me glumly, as we sorted through the data sets: "This one is empty. And that one. That one is corrupted, and this one doesn't even exist," he would say.

The value of the business that HMTF had assembled for €200m was, in reality, much less. I told one of the investment partners that it would be hard to make a commercial product from this data without investment – and was informed that they knew they had paid a strong price for the businesses and therefore such investment was not about to happen. I suggested to him that the owners were expecting me to "take off in Zurich (where we were based) in an old Dakota with one engine working and next to no fuel, with a team who don't really want to go on a flight anyway, and fly to Dallas (where HMTF were based). During the flight I am expected to pilot the plane, re-engineer it into Boeing 747, refuel it in mid-air, and train the flight crew to give excellent service."

He laughed and said, "yep, you got it".

We all knew the potential value of data in the auto business, especially when used to support purchasing decisions. It's just that the data we had wasn't the data we needed. We had to find a plan B, and somehow turn the data that we actually did have into useful intelligence. This is the point at which you really need someone, somewhere, to step up and be a genius.

Geniuses are made, not born

The idea that geniuses are somehow a separate race of people, genetically programmed to be extraordinary, does not stand up to analysis. According to Professor Michael Howe of Exeter University, who literally wrote the book on geniuses,[1] the people we consider to have genius have a lot in common with everyone else, but they just find a way to use their skills better. "Genuine creative achievements depend more on perseverance over the long haul than on prodigious childhood skills. We cannot all be geniuses but we can learn from them," he was telling the annual dinner of the British Psychological Society[2] around the time that I was sitting in an office in Zurich, wondering what to do next.

Howe's insight into genius is helpful. Although they have talent, their gift becomes extraordinary because they struggle hard and persist. They enjoy what they do, because they have (either by accident or on purpose) been placed in an environment that lets them flourish. They possess a sense of direction and purpose, and a commitment that allows them to resist distractions.

Even if your team is unlikely to be incubating the next Charles Darwin, this is exactly the sort of environment that we are attempting to create. It is precisely the environment, according to the research on what creates a genius, that has enabled creative ideas to emerge for hundreds of years.

In a business environment, many of the great geniuses started at the bottom. Michael Faraday, who invented the electric motor among hundreds of other experimental discoveries, was the self-taught son of a blacksmith who had little formal education. Benjamin Franklin, an inventor who pioneered research into electricity, had two years of schooling and ran away from home to work in a printer's shop.

Many great inventors (like William Glass) succeeded because of their ability to resist distractions when they were inspired to solve a problem.

Edwin Land, who among other firsts invented the Polaroid camera, would sometimes work for 36 hours straight when he had a challenge to overcome. He'd realize he'd been working for that long because he felt faint when he stood up. Famously, Thomas Edison told us that genius "was ninety-nine per cent perspiration and one per cent inspiration". He should know: he would commonly work for 112 hours a week.[3]

So, a sense of purpose is important in fostering bright ideas, as we saw in Chapters 1 and 2. As an inspiring leader, the structure you create that gives a voice to those ideas is vital (Chapters 5 and 6). You can't have all the best ideas, but you can push the genius of the people around you as far as it can go.

If you want to find your team's genius, then "we don't do that around here" isn't the way to start. When something that's clearly an improvement emerges, your genius is to recognize it, and use it.

Think different

At this point in the EurotaxGlass's story, it wouldn't have been difficult to find an improvement. It was clear that the fastest way to accelerate the value of the firm was to move from data to intelligence, but that's easy to say, and harder to do.

There were still a lot of people who didn't understand the value in data, but we knew that, if we could find a fit between what we knew and what the market wanted, it would be powerful. We considered buying the data from black boxes that are fixed in cars, or using traffic mapping data. From the companies we owned we had strong technical data and good sales data, service data, maintenance data and parts pricing data that we could combine in a continuous data set.

We thought we could create something for a dealer sales force that would show day to day what was happening in the market; what was selling, what the stock was, what price trends were, what demand was. But that was still data, without much added value. Jurgen's genius was to be the person who could understand how to make this data into a tool that would save businesses millions of euros. His genius insight was to understand the economic importance of depreciation in the auto sector – especially when linked to the new vehicle finance and funding offers that the vehicle manufacturers and their finance companies were so keen to bring to market.

Half the cost of owning your car is the money you lose as its value declines, year on year. Very few assets cost as much, compared to their value, before you even use them. A car depreciates in value faster than a computer. If you buy a new car today, it will, on average, have lost 60% of its value three years from now.[4]

Meanwhile, more than half of new car sales are to the fleet market. There were 16 million new car registrations in Europe in 2015. Fleet and business registrations made up approximately 50% of them.

This is a huge investment: in Europe, about €3.2 billion is lost to depreciation every year, and this is the risk that fleet operators carry. Minimizing this by using smart purchasing decisions would be a huge benefit to them. The manufacturers couldn't do much once they had created their cars: they were competing for this business by offering service incentives and £5 off a set of tyres, but – as Jurgen pointed out – compared to 60% of the value, it wasn't much of an incentive to switch brands. We had all the data to track how depreciation affected the value of new cars in incredible detail, in every country in which we did business: we knew demand for various used models, the prices charged in different markets and the differences in demand across Europe. But how could we use this to help buyers make decisions?

When I was at BMW, one of the things we were good at was packaging. This meant that you got to choose exactly the car you wanted: the type of seats, the radio, the finish, the sunroof. These small changes, which might change the price of a car only slightly when new, had a huge effect in the second-hand market. A model with expensive or unusual options would lose more of its value, because it would be harder to find a buyer with the same taste in the area in which it was being sold. A middle-of-the-road classic model would cost less to buy new than a specialized customization, but in the second-hand market it would probably be worth more than a more elaborate, personalized, version.

This variation in pricing, we discovered, was the case throughout Europe, but everywhere in Europe had different tastes. Germans liked black wheels, not steel wheels. The Spanish didn't want to buy a cabriolet because it's usually so hot that they preferred air conditioning. In Scandinavia, if your second-hand car did not have a heated steering wheel, nobody would want it. We knew this from our data.

And this was Jurgen's genius: he was able to crunch the data to produce reports, per model, per country for fleet buyers on which specifications of which models would depreciate least. We could tell them not just the expected depreciation per model, but by colour, engine type and for every other option. This produced a clear recommendation for them not just on which model to buy, but how to package it, and what the value would be three years later.

Each report took a few days of his time, and we decided to sell them for €25,000 per model, per country, because the value of this decision-making tool to manufacturers and fleet buyers was enormous (remember the cost of depreciation was €3.2 billion per year). In our traditional business, we were selling our guides for €40 per month.

Using the same data, we created a new business called "The Eurotax-Glass's Market Intelligent Unit". And then we added an analyst, then two analysts, then we had five, and this unit had a major impact on repositioning the entire business from a "data" to an "intelligence" company. This made the business much more valuable to potential acquirers.

This wasn't in our plan. We had a need, we had some data and we had Jurgen. But the genius is in knowing the data and the market well enough to see what we had, and to see where that represented value. It was far from obvious, and impossible for anyone who didn't obsessively watch the data and the industry from the inside.

But thanks to allowing this idea to run and become a project, we could forecast future depreciation. We could recommend the specification for a fleet buyer who was purchasing many thousands of new cars, to buy for each model in each country. We could estimate precisely what the depreciation would be, and how much they could save. And this affected their cost of financing the purchase. This was a huge, immediate saving from which the fleet buyers and the second-hand market benefited, and from which the manufacturers who had the lowest depreciation also benefited.

The question, though, was: what would the actual results be in three years? The good news was: his forecasts were extremely accurate.

Where are your geniuses?

Jurgen's flash of genius was more important than the creation of a new product. Previously we had been the company that sends the monthly book to the salesmen. Suddenly Jurgen and I were required to turn up at the launch of the new model Volkswagen Golf, to speak immediately after Martin Winkerkorn, the CEO, in the presentation of the market pricing strategy to thousands of VW corporate clients.

We had been elevated from being a used car guide, to being the expert on the total cost of ownership in the auto business, by using the same assets as we had all along. Jurgen was not a natural leader, but he had a natural skill for data analysis. Few of us will employ the 5% of us that's a genius to create such a huge amount of value.

If I speak first at a conference, I always like to stay around, to see what the rest of the day is about. Sometimes members of the team catch me afterwards and say "We love what you talked about, but we would never be allowed to do that." I believe that there's far more value locked up in our teams than we know, because most leadership is not created to make genius. How can you help bright ideas flourish?

Have a process for capturing and evaluating ideas When McKinsey and Co surveyed companies on how well they innovated,[5] 70% of leaders said it was a top-three priority, but 65% were "somewhat", "a little" or "not at all" confident in their ability to innovate inside their teams. Fewer than one in five actively managed innovation.

In the businesses I work with, the ideas wall is a feature of every workplace. Anyone can write on it, every idea is considered. It doesn't matter where the idea has come from. There's no need to overcomplicate how you generate new ideas.

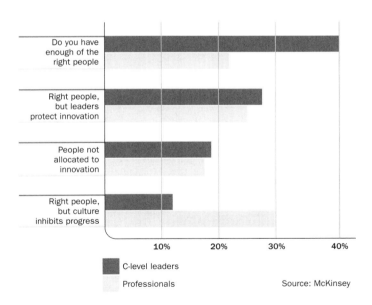

Ordinary people can achieve extraordinary results – make sure the culture allows the team to succeed

Tell your team that they have it in them Even worse, in the same study, leaders and their teams disagreed on what the problem was: 40% of leaders thought they didn't have the right people to innovate, while only 22% of professionals who reported to them thought the same. When asked whether the culture was the thing that was preventing innovation, only 12% of leaders agreed, but 30% of professionals who worked for them thought this was true.

Value the outcome I don't believe in suggestion schemes that give prizes for ideas: when I employ you, I expect to employ all of you, including your brain, when you are at work. But I do believe in sharing the benefit of your genius, giving you credit for it. An important part of that is to extract the value from genius: it's not enough to be clever, you have to package it in a way that meets a market need, or creates a new need. Jurgen's reports weren't just clever applications of data – they were clever applications that we could value at many times the price of our existing products. Within three years, they had become 10% of the turnover of the business and an even bigger part of our profitability.

The ideas wall and day counter in the cafe area at Fairline Boats

Being able to show the team how their genius has saved time or money, or created a new source of revenue, makes it easier for the team to recognize the value of great ideas. This is a far more profound incentive than the short-term pleasure of a prize for the best idea.

Never settle for 3% We are ruled by the fear of being different. The challenge is creating the shift to a new state. Wherever the resistance comes from, inspiring leaders should spend a lot of time (I do) convincing people not to try and slow us down when there are bright ideas that can change the business, even though they may initially seem a bit odd. Even if they are half right, chances are we will have growth far ahead of what we would otherwise have had.

Hire for attitude, train for skill Long interviews based on a list of past achievements aren't necessarily going to find the people who have bright ideas, imagine new ways to look at what you do, or show the commitment to solve a problem when others give up. You can help a problem-solver learn new skills. (And some of the most interesting creative minds, like Jurgen, can be hard to manage.)

It is natural for investors and managers to be scared by rapid change, but when they worry about where their next bright idea is coming from, sometimes they should look at their teams, and ask themselves what would happen if one of them was a secret genius. Many businesses can't innovate because they aren't encouraging the innovators they already employ. It is your job to create the commitment and environment that makes that change possible. When you do, the history of genius suggests that your next bright idea might come from an unlikely place.

Notes

1. Howe, M. 2001. *Genius Explained*. Cambridge, UK: Cambridge University Press.
2. Hartley-Brewer, J. 2000. Geniuses made with hard work, not born, *The Guardian*, 14 April.

3. Lykken, D. 1998. The genetics of genius. In A. Steptoe, *Genius and the Mind: Studies of Creativity and Temperament: Studies of Creativity and Temperament in the Historical Record*. Oxford, UK: Oxford University Press.
4. Source: The AA.
5. Barsh, J., Capozzi, M. and Davidson, J. 2008. Leadership and innovation, *McKinsey Quarterly* (January).

Chapter 9

Be Better First, Then Bigger

BEGIN AT THE END

Connect your vision to how you behave as a team *by describing success in 360 degrees*

A SIMPLE PLAN

Focus on the projects and priorities that make your vision real *by creating your 1,000-day plan*

Prepare for success

CONNECT

Everyone creates change

Sustain momentum

DON'T BE A GENIUS, MAKE A GENIUS

Uncover creativity that your team didn't know they had *by creating ways for bright ideas to flourish*

BE BETTER, THEN BIGGER

Inspire a world-class team *by emphasizing quality, not profit*

Companies often chase an arbitrary number when they think of their plan for the future. They try to grow sales to $100 million, or earn net profits of 12%, for example. I tell the teams I lead not to do that. Instead, focus on being better, and bigger will follow.

The dream of being world class at your job, whether that job is running the company or answering the telephone, has meaning and power for everyone. But you can't inspire a team just by targeting profit or market share or ROCE or RONA or any other management buzzword, because for most team members those are meaningless, abstract ideas that make very little difference to how they live and work.

So far, we have emphasized that inspired teams work best when they are striving to be the best. But, what is "best"? We might assume that everyone we work with shares our idea of terms like quality and world class.

In this chapter, I'll explain a little about the dimensions of quality that I experience. At the end of it you can apply those ideas to your team, because defining what "better" means to you can fundamentally change how team members view work. Being the best you can be should not be an abstract goal, but an inspiring way to live and work.

Being better is a state of mind

Chasing market share without improving quality is less than a zero-sum game. You sell harder, offer discounts and cut prices, and win 3% more of the market. Then your competitor matches your prices and discounts, and cuts a bit more. You lose that 3%. Everything is the same as before, except that you've both lost margin and created less loyal customers. At worst, you're in a race to the bottom.

While many companies will claim to have some sort of sustainable advantage, the truth is often more mundane. McKinsey Global Institute[1] produced a guide to British manufacturing, which it split into five categories. At the top of the list, innovative producers with a genuine competitive edge. Then strongly branded products (Scotch whisky, Burberry). Locational producers, which need to be close to markets, were third. "Exposed" producers – firms whose poor quality or technology made them vulnerable – and cost-based producers were the fourth and fifth categories.

McKinsey estimated that the first group represented 9% of our manufacturing employment, and the second group 5%. The bottom two categories, exposed to price competition, account for 64% of British manufacturing business.

There's only one way to avoid this trap, and that's to be better in some inspiring way.

A lot of teams think that's what they are doing already, but the 3% rule applies here too. Challenge your team to describe what they think you could do better, and some will start their answer by telling you, "I want a more accurate x" or, "I want to do this faster". Instinctively, we think about gradual change.

If we think differently, with a clear vision of success and all our actions aligned to that vision, then those small, incremental changes in how you can do things may add up to something bigger. This is the theory behind the "aggregation of marginal gains" which created Sir Dave Brailsford's revolution in British cycling. As he says, the 1% margin for improvement in everything you do can lead to a revolutionary change. In Brailsford's case, researching the pillow that was best for the cyclists to sleep on, and taking it to every hotel on the Tour de France route, or teaching riders the best way to wash their hands to avoid infection (don't miss out the thumbs). The point is that "better" is the aggregation of these marginal gains in the service of a bigger idea. Brailsford's dream wasn't for his riders to be 3% quicker. Brailsford had targeted a win in the Tour in five years for a British rider. He succeeded in three.

If we find ourselves using money, or market share, to measure what "better" is, we think small. When I ask teams to dream, it's disappointing to hear: "We want to be a $100 million company."

"You're limiting yourself," I tell them, "That number's just a limit."

The best internet companies, who don't need to build factories and employ salespeople to grow, show the power of doing what it is to be the best. Google's 2000 revenue in its first full year of business was $19.1 million. In 2001, its second full year, this jumped to $86.4 million. It grew by 352% at a time when people were wondering how it could make any money at all. But, if its goal had been to be an $86.4 million company, it would have succeeded. Instead, its goals were to be better at internet search, at using information, or at artificial intelligence than anyone else. When they achieved their goal to be better, extraordinary growth came naturally.

The difference is that this type of "better" isn't an incremental improvement. It's a fresh way to look at the challenge you face.

Being better means thinking big

It is rare, and exciting, to work in a team who consider the idea of being "better" as creating something completely different. Here's an example from a startup called delvv.io that I'm currently working with.

You have probably heard the following quote: "Half the money I spend on advertising is wasted; the trouble is I don't know which half." This was said by John Wanamaker, who ran department stores at the end of the 19th century. It might surprise you to know that the brightest minds in the market research industry, a business worth £4 billion in the UK alone,[2] are still a long way from solving Wanamaker's problem. The market research business earns a lot from helping discover whether advertising is working. They should. In the UK, advertisers spend £18 billion a year (and in the US, the figure is $190 billion).[3] So we can say that the industry knows that £9 billion of what it spends is wasted.

Clearly, marginal gains to cut £9 billion (or $95 billion) of waste are welcome. But what are the opportunities if we can radically rethink the quality of advertising?

To for advertisers, "quality" in market research means being able to make better decisions. They can make some gains from learning more about their audiences, or from their previous advertising campaign. But imagine if they could avoid making mistakes in the campaigns before they ran the ads? That's why advertisers pre-test their ideas.

Traditionally, this testing is conducted through a focus group or a quantitative survey. Both techniques rely on groups, also known as panels, of consumers. Almost all companies do pre-testing, because it can pick out large errors early – for example, if no one gets the joke.

It has been possible to improve re-testing in marginal ways: for example, by providing a bigger panel, advertisers can find out if it appeals to different segments of the population. Different types of questions can be asked. Some advertisers prefer to use technology such as eye-tracking or measuring brainwaves to discover the public's response.

But, whatever the technology, there are also problems with this approach. Not least because an idea that could be good gets thrown out for the wrong reasons. Maybe the tagline isn't quite right, or the artwork should have a different style. Importantly, consumers sometimes approve advertising that's a bit like what they know. Some innovators in advertising (for example, Nike) refuse to pre-test ideas for exactly this reason.

Two entrepreneurs called Trevor Wolfe and Remon Geyser came to me in 2016 with a completely different idea of how to be better, and a company called delvv.io to do it. delvv.io's idea was to improve the quality of the development process by creating a community of professionals to give feedback. The advertiser or the agency upload creative concepts, delvv.io matches the work with the 30 most relevant professionals and, within seven days, the advertiser gets a report on strengths and weaknesses, with recommendations on how to improve it.

This offers both an entirely new way for advertisers to improve, but also the possibility of new ways to think about the creative process. Advertisers who need instant advice, and are willing to pay for it, can dip into delvv.io's "Facebook of creatives" and get a response in as little as 20 minutes. Instead of spending time presenting creative work, the response can automatically be made into a presentation by delvv.io's systems, with all the analysis and feedback, that's better than 80% of the hand-crafted presentations I've seen.

Trevor and Remon have, in 12 months, won Unilever, L'Oréal, Barclays, FNB, Pernod Ricard, OUTSurance and GSK, among others, as clients, because they understood what "better" was for the people they do business with, and they were not scared to try to solve the problem in a completely different way.

Our dream is to build the world's biggest marketing services company. There are thousands of providers who are bigger but none that are better at what we do.

Being better is about everything you do

Wherever your customer touches your brand, that customer should get the same experience. The second point about being better is that you must be *consistently* better. When you put all your effort into improving in one dimension, but ignore the others, then it's hard to move the needle on how others see you.

Apple's packaging is exquisite, because that signals the care with which the product has been designed and made. They spend so much time on the packaging because that's the first thing people touch.

That attention to detail is a sign of quality in itself. And those details are easy to miss in our own teams, because we don't often look at ourselves, and ask honestly how others experience what we do. We tend to focus on internal measures of quality, which tend to be driven by our own processes. There's no point in answering calls quickly in a call centre if the operators don't give the best advice when customers get through. But because one is easy to measure, and the other often harder, the internal measurement tends to be used as "better".

Take a company called ITS Technology Group that I'm working with, as an example. They provide broadband for hard-to-reach rural and urban businesses, communities and regions, closing the digital divide. The quality of the engineers and the technology that our engineers provide is extraordinary, and we can measure the quality by testing the strength of a wi-fi signal or the speed of a connection. We're already a very good provider, but we can always ask our engineers to make us better in those dimensions, though not so much better that most customers would notice.

But, recently, we also tested the quality of the technical support. When you call, as with almost any other technology company, you get a list of options: "Press 1 for . . ." At ITS, we realized that our clients couldn't work out which number to press. The reason was that the categories had been designed by the same group of engineers, who knew the answers already. What was good enough for them was certainly not the quality that users expected.

Our internal measures of quality aren't always obvious for the customer – especially for a company like ITS. At ITS, when the product works, no one notices it. Most of the time when customers come into contact with ITS, they are looking for help, and may be frustrated and confused. If they are confronted with a system which is not designed to make it simple for them to resolve their problem, that poor experience may influence their opinion of the entire brand. In the instant that they communicate with the company a poor response hurts the relationship but, if it is bad enough, they will tell their friends about it, and that will hurt even more. In quality, the little things matter. At ITS we modified the telephone system.

A powerful example of how successful companies forget what it means to be better comes from the US truck business. Toyota (more about this company later) is synonymous with quality in manufacturing. It was one of the companies that brought "Total Quality Management" (TQM) to the auto industry, and is the second-largest manufacturer of cars in the world, after the Volkswagen Group.

Today we hear the phrase "the voice of the customer" (VoC) as something that sales and marketing use to measure public opinion or satisfaction. For Japanese companies like Toyota, every department had the job of listening to that voice. For decades its cars have been designed by asking customers how they should improve, or finding out what made customers unhappy with their products.

By the turn of the century, in the US, GM and Ford had long dominated the truck business. Ranchers and farmers were conservative, and preferred not to change brands. But GM and Ford built quality into some parts of their business (powerful engines, for example) but not others (some parts rusted quickly). When Toyota redesigned its Tundra truck, instead of targeting all truck owners and asking them, the company concentrated on the most serious users. Those users influenced others, their research showed. They visited "truck graveyards" to find which parts had rusted through, and went to ranches to watch truck owners working. They found that ranchers loved all the things about American trucks that the manufacturers thought they did – but also had a long, detailed list of smaller complaints that no one had thought to ask about. One example: when you build a truck for ranchers who wear thick gloves to work, they would prefer it if you put a bigger tuning knob on the radio.

This, and hundreds of other improvements, made the Tundra not just better than the previous model, but recognized as far superior to American trucks by the users. A few years later it became, from nowhere, the market leader.

Being better is not about spending money

Price is not a number, it's an experience. If the service is not correct, you feel aggrieved, whatever you pay. You are disappointed.

This is one of the many aspects of inspirational leadership that is about out-thinking, not outspending. Being better can also mean being cheaper, but too many companies would say "save the money". Provided the business is financially stable, I prefer to provide an extraordinary experience, because ultimately, I believe that is what will generate greater commercial success.

But lower price and improved products and services are not mutually exclusive. By thinking smarter at Fairline about how we could pre-build some parts of the boats we made, we took 20% out of the cost of building a boat. That's an improvement in two ways. First, with the pre-built units the boats were of a higher manufactured quality. But just as significant was the effect these improvements had on a company that was starved of cash. We could invest in other key strategic areas, for example in designing a new boat. Saving money was a way to improve the overall quality of what we did, not an end in itself.

Similarly, at Porsche we urgently needed a car that would sell for less than £29,000, for sales tax reasons. At the time, the Porsche 968 was £36,000. We needed a less expensive Porsche, but no one wants a cheap Porsche – we had to think differently, about how it would be both the right price, and somehow represent higher quality for that type of driver. And so we created the 968 Club Sport.

The Club Sport was a Porsche with all the frills taken out. No electric windows. No central locking, No leather seats. They were available in white, black, yellow, red and blue. The car was 100kg lighter because we had cut down on some of the heavy components, so it had improved performance and handling.

We had set out to build a £29,000 Porsche, but instead created something that matched the brand aspirations of a group of customers who loved it – and still do. It won "Performance Car of the Year" from *Autocar* magazine in the UK. It cost less than £29,000, but wherever you touched that car, it was true to the Porsche brand experience.

Being better is everyone's job, all the time

Henry Ford said: "Quality means doing it right when no one is looking." The final point about being better isn't just a product or a service, it's a way of life for the whole team. It's the guiding principle for how you achieve every dream you set yourselves. You definitely need to measure marginal gains, cost savings, product quality and productivity. But if you only inspire people to do better when you're measuring them, your team is missing the point.

Passion, enthusiasm, inclusion and engagement are the keys to quality, but that applies to everyone. If your task as an inspiring leader is to create a vapour trail in the sky, everyone in the business needs a line of sight too: they have to see the value of their commitment to quality in the way you lead.

**

It was Easter Sunday in the early 1990s, my first year in charge at Porsche Cars GB. We'd set ourselves a goal for everyone, at all times, to provide world-class service, at every point. But it was Sunday and so, of course, I was in the office, because the business was close to collapse and, apparently, I had volunteered to fix it. Dave, in security, phoned me, partly because he was the only other person in the building. "There are two people poking their nose through the fence looking at the cars," he told me.

The young married couple weren't doing anything wrong (we had 300 unsold cars sitting in the car park at the time, arguably no one would have noticed if they actually had driven off in one). They had just always wanted to buy a Porsche, and had come to have a look, but we didn't have a retail shop at head office at the time.

I said, "Invite them in, Dave," and I brought them to my office and made them a cup of tea. They had never sat in a Porsche, they said, but were keen to buy one. So we finished our tea, and I took them down to the workshop, flicked all the lights on, and we sat in the cars. I walked round with them for an hour, showed them everything we had.

I couldn't take them out for a test drive, but I took their name and address, and arranged a test drive for them the following week. Then I went back to the pile of work on my desk.

The following week, my press officer told me I was in *AutoCar*. Not quoted talking about Porsche this time. I was letter of the week: my new friends had written in, and, in glowing terms, described their experience and how special we had made them feel. I would expect that if anyone else in my management team had been in, they would have done exactly the same thing.

Both Dave and I were proud to have given our guests a special Porsche experience. Pride in your job is not embarrassing. Pride in a job done well creates quality at every level. When it came to creating an image of quality at Porsche for visitors, the security men and the cleaners were literally among the most important people in the business.

When you came into Porsche head office, there were four pristine cars sitting on a shiny atrium floor which was slightly elevated so that you could clearly see under the cars. Some people gossiped that Porsches dripped oil. None of our cars dripped more than cars from any other manufacturer, but all cars drip oil. We fretted that people would come into reception, and the first thing they would note wouldn't be four shiny, beautiful, quality cars. They would see four patches of oil.

Somebody said: "We'll put a drip tray under that." But drip trays would have said that we accept that we drip oil. So, the cleaners agreed to check every day, twice a day, that there would never be oil on the floor. People complimented us on how clean our offices were, and drivers noticed that there were no drips under our cars. The cleaners did that. They owned the Porsche brand experience as much as I did.

Getting better doesn't just mean being more luxurious, or more comfortable, or using thicker paper, or deeper paint. It means being appropriate to what that client expects of the brand. That's a different perception. It doesn't mean just fixing the things you think are important. It means that all the details, from everyone, all the time add up to something that achieves your vision of what you could be, because quality is doing it right when no one is looking.

Big visions matter – but the small details matter just as much.

Notes

1. Manyika, J. 2012. *Manufacturing the Future*. London: McKinsey Global Institute.
2. Source: Market Research Society. The figure is for 2015.
3. Source: Statista.com.

Chapter 10

In Command,
Out of Control

BEGIN AT THE END

Connect your vision to how you behave as a team *by describing success in 360 degrees*

A SIMPLE PLAN

Focus on the projects and priorities that make your vision real *by creating your 1,000-day plan*

IN COMMAND, OUT OF CONTROL

Lead and inspire without micromanaging *by trusting your sense of shared purpose*

Prepare for success

CONNECT

Everyone creates change

Sustain momentum

DON'T BE A GENIUS, MAKE A GENIUS

Uncover creativity that your team didn't know they had *by creating ways for bright ideas to flourish*

BE BETTER, THEN BIGGER

Inspire a world-class team *by emphasizing quality, not profit*

The most powerful words in the business aren't necessarily spoken, they are understood.

The previous chapters have emphasized the importance of planning, and of following a process when you connect your vision of change to the business. But decisions constantly have to be made along the way, and unexpected problems constantly show up.

In this chapter, we will look at why it is vital that you trust your team to move fast and make decisions for themselves. They may make mistakes if they cannot be avoided, but we will look at how to learn fast from them and fix them. To do this, you need to create a culture in which everyone has trust and everyone understands their role.

The plan, and the way you manage the plan, is our guide to making the impossible possible. The daily detail of how we get there relies on the ability of everyone, not just you, to manage themselves.

Out of control is natural (and good)

The title comes from the military: "command and control" is what we imagine military leadership does. In 2002, General Paul van Riper of the US Marines memorably undermined this idea in a US military wargame using sophisticated computer simulations, called "Millennium Challenge '02", which accidentally became a national news story when the US Army managed to defeat itself. Van Riper had been picked to command Red Team in the exercise (the enemy). He was acting as a rogue general in the Persian Gulf who was in command of terrorist groups, and who had threatened to destabilize the entire region. Against him, Blue Team – the US Military, and its expensive analytical capability designed to control the situation.

Blue Team were convinced that they could win easily by cutting Red Team's communications. Instead, van Riper used improvisation, messages delivered by hand, and techniques borrowed from the Second World War to get coded information to his team, who were instructed to make their own decisions while following the plan, acting on the minimum of data. On day two of the exercise, Red Team managed to launch a surprise missile attack on the US fleet out of the blue, and sank it. If it had been a real war, 20,000 people would have been killed in the attack.[1]

The response of the US military was to run the wargame again, but this time with a script that Red Team had to follow, so Blue Team could win using its computer system. ("In the 41 years that I was on active duty I never saw anything as dysfunctional and dishonest as this particular exercise," van Riper said later.) A few months after this it launched Desert Storm, which showed the problems of relying on central control. In the first 30 hours of the operation, the US military sent 1.3 million emails.

Van Riper, after he retired from the military, argued that this dysfunction was the culmination of a centuries-long process of trying to assert complete centralized control. This began as soon as warfare became too complex for someone to direct by looking at his army from the top of a hill. First armies used messengers on foot, then on horseback, invented semaphore, used the telegraph and, finally, computers in an attempt to exert control from wherever command was located. But they were always playing catch up, because a greater number of unexpected things happen, more rapidly, than any system of reporting can handle. This doesn't just apply to warfare, he adds.

"We normally think 'out of control' is something bad'," van Riper said, "but a modern business is inherently uncertain and complex. Accept the world as it is, and learn to operate in spite of uncertainty. We live in an uncertain and changing world, and unexpected things happen and we have unexpected results."

There is a danger that, as an inspiring leader, the structure that the planning process puts on the business can tempt you to micromanage, to try to stay in control of every tiny problem. But, if this happens, you suffocate your team. They often know what to do without writing you a report, and in most cases how to fix day-to-day problems. You are on this journey because you have the same vision. You have told them that you have confidence in their ability to create world-class performance. This is the test of whether you really believe this is true.

Planning is about the clarity of a vision of success, the clarity of objectives, and about ensuring that all of the training, culture and attitude are aligned with the pursuit of that vision of success. You can make sure the briefing is accurate. Make sure people know what is expected of them. Make sure people are trained, equipped and have the right attitude. Check that you've got the skills you need in the team. Define what success is for each 50-day project.

But then step back and let the team go.

When there's a team of people walking to the South Pole where the flat, featureless terrain makes navigation difficult we walk in a single file. The person at the front has taken a bearing and set off walking. The rest follow, but who is in charge of navigation? It's whoever is at the back. When you trust your team to do the work, that's where you should be, because only that person can see if the group is veering off course. Everyone else can keep walking.

Teams solve your problems

An example, from Fairline Boats. The London Boat Show, held at the ExCel Exhibition Centre every January, was one of the biggest events of the year for Fairline. With 300 exhibitors, it is both an opportunity to do business and a place to show off to future customers and the press. Companies gear their entire marketing plan around the show, and spend hundreds of thousands of pounds to create giant displays and launch new boats.

We had a tenth of that budget, and nothing to launch. I took over as CEO in September 2013, and the show opened on 4 January 2014. We had to decide what we were going to put on the stand. We couldn't drop out. It was the biggest event of the year and our biggest marketing expense of the year by far. By this stage, journalists had been writing consistently negative stories about Fairline for months. They were telling us we had lost our way, predicting we would soon be going out of business. The Boat Show would demonstrate if we knew what we were doing. I had been to plenty of car shows in the past, so I knew how important they are to set the tone, and convince press and customers to talk about the future of Fairline, not its past.

Having organized a show stand 15 times or so before, my natural reaction could have been to start micromanaging and forcing my opinion on everyone else. I was determined that this would be the team's show, their chance to shine. So 15 of us got together, and we had a discussion about what we were going to put on the stand.

The team knew the show – they had been there often enough. They knew what it was like to visit, and who would be there. They knew what was exciting, and what was boring, and what should be different this year. They wanted to create an experience, from beginning to end, that was unique in the show.

We had a discussion about which boats we were going to take. Our competitor Princess would be showing its new 43. Sunseeker would bring its 75 Yacht, and had booked James Corden to show it to the press. We had a newish design, but it was still three years old. When we were reduced to talking about how we could show a boat with a slightly different deck and some new colour schemes, we all realized we needed a bigger idea.

I asked the design director to think about a new boat. This was an exciting brief for him. He had sketches of some ideas he had been experimenting with for ordinary boats, working boats, but I knew from my time at motor shows that people loved the concept cars that we built, featuring the most advanced technologies and unusual design. We decided we needed a concept boat, to his design. "Give me something that will make the journalists go, 'wow'," was the brief I gave him.

And he came back and he said, "I think we've got it."

The design for the Fairline eSprit, which his team had conjured from my nine-word brief, looked magnificent. It was "a glimpse of the future of luxury motor boating". It was, in the words of our marketing department:

". . . an exciting proposition for the future of sustainable motor boating, without compromising Fairline's class-leading styling and performance . . .

The Fairline eSprit incorporates sustainable materials in construction and design. Bio-derived epoxy resins with needle punched flax fibres are used in construction and the interior features ecoyarn upholstery fabrics, specially treated with a waterproofing plasma process. Recycled synthetic teak is used for the eSprit's decking and the concept incorporates a solar panelled T-top that folds away to cover bow seating when not in use . . .

The concept boat showcases an ergonomically optimised interior and includes a Multifunctional Steering Position with paddle throttles and integral LED control display. This allows chartplotter, radar and system information to be displayed in the optimum viewing position . . ."

"This is the budget to build it," he said, showing me a figure.

"We haven't got that much money for building prototypes," I told him.

"How much have you got?" he asked.

"Nothing," I said.

Our designer had contributed his genius, but how could we show a boat that doesn't exist?

"We could do it in CGI," said a young guy at the back of the group, "it wouldn't cost much." So that's what we decided to do: build a virtual boat.

As the show approached, the team's stand looked magnificent. We had found the world's biggest union flags, and draped them over our 50-foot boats. The team planned to whip them off to reveal our boats to the press, but they had changed the way they did that too. Normally the press conferences were at 8am, before the public were allowed in. But anyone who has met the journalists knows that they hate travelling to East London for a bacon sandwich in an empty exhibition hall at 8am. So the team had planned our reveals at 11am, in front of both press and a public audience. Our marketing manager had used his contacts to get access to the big screens in ExCel to show our eSprit video, so every time a competitor wanted to show off its design, our concept boat would be behind it, music pounding.

My sales and marketing director, Stuart, was an experienced sailor and a boat show veteran. He came to see the stand the night before and walked around carefully, with a boater's eye. He called me over to the lounge area and pointed at our largest boat. "Boaters will spot that," he said, pointing at the hull of the boat. You could clearly see that it had a ripple in its hull caused by a small fault in the moulding process. We hadn't noticed it before because the show stand had been full of stand builders and scaffolding. Given time we could have repaired it but we didn't have time. This was the only boat we had available. We couldn't polish it out, and the boat is as big as a house, so you couldn't miss it if you sat in the Fairline lounge area. The next day it would look worse as it would have stage lighting on it.

Stuart said he would fix it. I had no idea how, but I trusted him to find a way. In the morning when I walked onto the stand I saw that Stuart had taken a beautiful potted tree, and put it next to the boat so that the ripple was hidden. Problem solved. Don't outspend, outthink.

The Fairline team who achieved extraordinary results at the national boat show

At the show, Fairline's staff had transformed the boat show experience. They built a cinema underneath the show stand. You had to queue to go in, with the music we had created booming from it. There were beautiful backlit graphics. Inside the cinema, at punishing volume, they got to see a video[2] in which the computer-generated eSprit was revealed from beneath a 3D-graphics union flag. It glided across an imaginary ocean. "Fairline also announced its plans for a 30ft hybrid sports boat, the eSprit, which Fairline says it is judging interest before deciding to put it in production," *Motorboat & Yacht* magazine reported the next day.

Outside the cinema, the team had decided on another innovation: to take away the barriers that separate the visitors from the boats. "You're welcome to come and sit in our boats,"[3] they told the public.

At that show, for an outlay that was a fraction of the money spent by similar brands, we outsold our nearest competitor two to one. The lesson I learn every time I work with a team is that, as an inspiring leader, the best way you can inspire people is to trust them to get on with it. Give them a clear brief, set the standards, make sure everybody knows, and then get out of their way.

Good leaders delegate

"Our first accomplishments as professionals are usually rooted in our skill as individual contributors. In most fields we add value in the early stages of our careers by getting things done. We're fast, we're efficient, and we do high-quality work. In a word, we're doers," says Ed Batista, an executive coach and an Instructor at the Stanford Graduate School of Business. "But when we carry this mindset into our first leadership roles, we confuse doing with leading. We believe that by working longer, harder, and smarter than our team, we'll inspire by example."

He argues that, while the functional skills such as accounting and finance can be recruited, they don't often add to the effectiveness of a team. Being the person who creates the environment in which they can work together is a tougher, rarer skill.

I passionately believe that. This is why I say that the loudest words in our business are not spoken, but they are understood, because it means that people can manage themselves by asking: "What does Kevin expect?", or even better "How good can we make this?" Most people in your team are overworked but underutilized. We all need people who will do the hard work, but who we can also trust to do the job.

But we all say we want to delegate, that we are too busy, and then find ourselves lost in detail at 2am. Sydney Finkelstein is a professor of management and Director of the Leadership Center at the Tuck School of Business at Dartmouth College. He closely followed 200 leaders who are good delegators to discover how they did it.[4] He discovered the habits of good delegators:

They live to invent Change is the natural state of business for these leaders, so you give your team permission to change things that aren't right. That's the point of the ideas wall in the businesses that I work with. He describes Jay Chiat, who created the advertising agency Chiat/Day, which made some of the most innovative advertising of the 20th century. "If you came to Jay with an idea for how things could be done better, he would say, 'Go ahead and do it.'"

The flip side of this is that, in an "out of control" world, mistakes will be made. Recall the research that 2–5% of mistakes deserve blame, but that 70–90% were treated as blameworthy? It doesn't matter how much you delegate if you shoot the messenger when it goes wrong, because employees will be scared to take the initiative you give them. Brief properly, monitor, but you can't manage failure out of existence.

They understand their employees As I mentioned, when I joined BMW I shocked my PA by deciding to walk around the business, to visit staff where they worked and ask them how they were doing, instead of waiting for them to book an appointment to see me. When you do this, you get a sense for what is happening, you can ask questions without calling a meeting, and you break down the barriers that would genuinely keep you out of the loop. This can lead to more delegation, because you become a colleague, not a job title.

They have clear boundaries Everything can be delegated, *except the vision*. "These leaders articulate uncompromising visions that they expect employees to internalize and follow. During the execution of work tasks, employees enjoy extraordinary authority over everything *except* the vision," Finkelstein explains.

This isn't just ego. The vision is shared. It is a group commitment. So, if one of the team members departs from the vision – and I have seen this from time to time with people who refuse to change the way they do business – it undermines everyone. This is also a source of strength: knowing exactly what decisions they can make, the team also knows exactly where their autonomy ends. Which means that they can still be decisive, where it counts and within the agreed limits.

There is also a practical reason to delegate. If you don't, you will probably make a lot of bad decisions. The first person to notice this in business was Friedrich von Hayek, an economist during the middle of the 20th century, who studied how command economies such as the old Soviet Union worked – or didn't. Trying to be an all-powerful central planner could never be the most efficient way to organize, he argued, because that planner can never know enough, at the right time. There is an inevitable trade-off between having all the information while being too late to act on it, or acting on the information you have, which is far less than the aggregated knowledge of the people at ground level who are reporting to you. He called it the *knowledge problem*.

He wrote[5] at the end of the Second World War: "It is rather a problem of how to secure the best use of resources known to any of the members of society, for ends whose relative importance only these individuals know."

We would all agree with this in principle. As we saw, 57 years later, the US Army forgot this lesson and built a system to try to solve the knowledge problem, and found that it generated 1.3 million emails that no one had time to read when they were in the middle of a battle.

Hayek argued that prices go some way to solving this problem when we're thinking about how an entire economy is organized, because in our economy no dictator needs to tell a company what to do with its product. The company decides for itself that if it runs out of stock because demand is high it should raise prices, or maybe find a way to make more.

But, if we try to extend this to how individual businesses work, there's a problem: when it comes to planning, companies are very often organized more like the Soviet Union than a market economy (it might not be a coincidence that, between 1928 and 1987, central planning delivered growth of a steady 3% every year for the Soviet Union's economy). Often those massive plans that sit in a cupboard have been created by a small elite group who are doing their best, but are too remote from what's actually going on. The plans are handed to employees who scratch their heads and wonder what to do with them, and perhaps decide that no one would notice if they just carried on doing the things they did before.

As an inspiring leader, when you make a plan you are doing something fundamentally different. You don't just decide what to put in the plan, you communicate your vision, and use prioritize, prioritize, prioritize to work with your team to decide what is the most effective way to achieve it. When you decide priorities together, each key priority has a position that represents its value to the team. This decision has been made by aggregating the knowledge of everyone in the room. So, while everyone might not agree with every detail, the plan that results makes sense and has legitimacy. Afterwards, you can have confidence when you delegate that the message make sense for both the future of the business and decisions that each project team will take, because the strategy was decided and agreed by everyone, based on what they know to be real and true. This is how you can use the collective knowledge of the business to minimize unnecessary day-to-day control, while staying in total command.

Keep the heartrate high

One of the most important challenges has to be to stop the team members settling back into the "now plus 3%" mentality when you are not in the room. This 3% may have been the dominant narrative in the business before you showed up, and if you're a team inside a larger business, it's probably the dominant story elsewhere in the business. So you can't blame some people for settling back into something that feels comfortable. You might be tempted to do it too. This is never good. When you give trust to the team, you are trusting them not to do this, because it undermines the vision. When this happens, the business might be running like clockwork, but clockwork isn't necessarily what you are looking for.

If you feel totally in control on day 864 of the plan, it's most likely that you're just not going fast enough.

Settling back is often a response to the uncertainty and risk of dealing with the outside world. In van Riper's words, the world in which we live is "inherently uncertain and complex". Therefore, if the heartbeat that you raised returns to normal, this isn't a healthy response. It actually means the opposite, because it makes it more likely that events will overtake you. So how do you balance delegation with inspiration?

Lead by exception Keep the war room in view – I prefer to put it somewhere I can see from my office. Make sure people go there, use it, see it and report on the projects that need reporting. Then, when you walk around and see which folders are red, you know that's where you direct your attention. Deal with it today. Resist the temptation to think: I'm sure it will be better next week. Give 100% of your leadership skills to the problems that need to be managed, and find out whether the failure can be avoided. If so, fix it quickly.

Don't forget the whinge wall When you started this adventure, that whinge wall was full. Many people were upset about many things in the business. But the team has worked well, and a year later it's empty. No one has anything to complain about.

It's a good story, but it is not a true story. Make sure that the whinge wall, however you want to collect the whinges, is active, and that the whinges are encouraged and listened to. These are the current spontaneous ideas coming back from the team. People get used to the status quo, but the status quo is your enemy: it means we stop noticing things at ground level that need to be changed, and which might destabilize the plan. So fix the whinges. These are typically frustrations or irritations which distract the team and waste energy. Address the issue, move on.

A 200-day review The plan is not a tablet of stone, so fix 200-day reviews. You have trusted the team – is there anywhere it isn't working? Is there a part of the business that needs to be in the plan, or a set of projects that aren't working? This is a full, formal review among the leadership team, not a quick spot check. You will want to change some things, maybe bring some ideas out of the birdcage. If everyone knows that there is a regular review, it not only helps to motivate them in what they do today, but stops the team wasting time when the situation changes.

One of my favourite business books isn't about a business at all: *It's Your Ship* is the story of Captain D. Michael Abrashoff,[6] and the practical but inspirational changes he made when he was in charge of USS Benfold. He placed signs everywhere on board that read "It's your ship" to inspire sailors under his command to use their nous and experience.

"Leaders must free their subordinates to fulfil their talents," he writes, "most obstacles that limit people's potential are rooted in the leader's own fears, ego and unproductive habits . . . If a rule doesn't make sense, break it!"

I firmly believe that, if we get planning right, we manage better when we manage less. One reason for this, as we will see in the final section, is that if you keep the heartrate high while building trust with your team, you find that you treat each other with more respect, unleash positivity and have more fun. You create magic.

Notes

1. Read about this in Gladwell, M. 2005. *Blink*. New York: Little, Brown.
2. You can watch it here: http://bit.ly/FLeSprit
3. This is something that we'd often used for car shows at Porsche, which worked well until we discovered someone unbolting one of the seats. "I'm just seeing how it comes out," he said. We politely asked him to put it back.
4. Finkelstein, S. 2016. *Superbosses*. New York: Portfolio Penguin.
5. Hayek, F. 1945. The use of knowledge in society, *The American Economic Review*. 35(4): 519–530.
6. Abrashoff, M. 2002. *It's Your Ship: Management Techniques from the Best Damn Ship in the Navy*. New York: Business Plus Books.

Part Three

Create

Chapter 11

Are We Having Fun Yet?

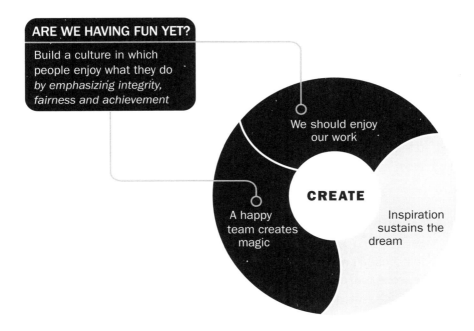

ARE WE HAVING FUN YET?

Build a culture in which people enjoy what they do *by emphasizing integrity, fairness and achievement*

We should enjoy our work

CREATE

A happy team creates magic

Inspiration sustains the dream

In the book so far we have investigated the idea of creating a dream, inspiring your team to find its motivation, and working with it to translate that motivation into work, day by day. I love seeing a team come together, working well and taking pleasure in what it is doing. That's what is behind the first two elements of what an inspirational leader does: you commit (and encourage others to do the same), and then you connect the dream to daily work and the 1,000-day plan.

But you will not be with your team for every one of those 1,000 days. You need to make sure that the energy that you have unlocked is channeled into achieving this vision. In the final section, we need to look at the character of the workplace that you create, so that it's a good place to be, and so that magic that you have created is sustained everywhere, all the time. Also, so that you can enjoy what you create.

The most important aspect of this is that your team has fun at work, and gets satisfaction from the job.

In this chapter, we will look at what "fun" means, why it is important for other reasons too, and what you as a leader can (and can't) do to create a fun workplace. At the end of it, you should be able to take the temperature of your team with regards to how much they are enjoying the journey as well as how much progress they have made.

Work is emotional

My idea of fun might not be yours. I love my work. Now I split my time between several companies. When I'm not visiting them, I work most of the time at home, in my office. In the morning I go to the gym, or drag tyres around for an hour or two, a habit I picked up when I was training to walk to the Poles, and then I'll start at about 10am, and I'm often still at my desk at 11pm. I keep telling my family I'll slow down, but I haven't yet.

Why not? Because, as they know, I'm addicted to the excitement of what these companies can achieve. I have been to some of the most extreme places on Earth, climbed mountains and jumped out of aeroplanes, but there's nothing better than the satisfaction of being part of a team that's creating something both worthwhile and amazing, and maybe achieving things that everyone (me included) thought would be impossible when we set out. When we actually see results, every day, then you don't need a spreadsheet to be inspired: you get it from looking at the faces of the people you work with.

We spend so much of our time describing what we do, abstracting it in spreadsheets and graphs, measuring it and telling each other about it in presentations, that sometimes we forget to experience the joy of what we make too, just as our customers are experiencing it. Sometimes it is harder than others, but if we truly believe that we are doing something that's extraordinary in our teams, why do we deny ourselves the chance to know how extraordinary it is? We can't work only in our heads, we have to feel the emotion.

I've been very fortunate in my career in that I've been given the chance to feel a connection to some inspiring products too. For example, as an engineer, there was no better place for me to be the boss than Porsche, where the cars fill you with excitement, inside and out.

But, when I became the leader, there was no joy on the faces of anyone working there, and part of that was because they didn't feel connected to what we did. The cars that we sold (and, at that time, were failing to sell) were just things that other people, who lived in another world, would drive.

This is not unusual. According to the Edenred Ipsos Barometer,[1] which is a survey of employees all over the world, the UK has an average level of job satisfaction: 71% of Brits are happy at work. Only Germany, where the figure is 74%, has happier employees in Europe. This isn't driven by big offices or an expensive computer – India, where hours of work are long and working conditions are less luxurious, has the world's most contented office workers. UK employees are happy that they have the tools to do their job, much more so than the average worker. On the other hand, they don't feel emotional engagement with their work. They don't think their job in interesting, and tend not to enjoy coming to work. This drags the average down. The same is true in the survey for most countries in advanced economies: we've created beautiful offices, but neglected to inspire the people who work in them.

When I had my chance to lead Porsche, the bottom had fallen out of the market. We had an entire field of unsold cars. Working in a failing business, if you don't relate to the thing the business sells, must have been doubly demoralizing for the staff.

So, one day early on, I had an idea: let them drive the cars.

We hired Millbrook Proving Ground in Bedfordshire, and brought some of our cars there, as well as all of our staff, to give them a taste of what they were working so hard to sell. If you watch Top Gear on TV, you will have occasionally seen Millbrook: built as a twisting, demanding circuit for manufacturers to test their new car designs, it's fun to drive. It's even more fun to drive behind the wheel of a Porsche 911 Carrera 4 with more than 300 horsepower, which goes from 0 to 60mph in just over 4 seconds.

It was the most fun of all if you had walked past these cars every day at work, but never so much as sat inside them.

In my first leadership job, I now realize that at Millbrook I road-tested one of the ideas that I have used ever since: give people in your team some freedom to explore and they'll start enjoying work they previously thought was boring. The crazy things that we decided to do, and post on the wall in our business plan, become an adventure. People come into work each day looking forward to making a difference.

You don't have to sell fast cars to connect your team with the product. It's the same logic that Tesco used to use for its senior managers. Sir Terry Leahy, the chief executive, had started off working in a Tesco store and every year he asked the leadership team to spend a week working in the business. Without telling customers who they were, they would help pack shopping at the till, or ride along on deliveries in a Tesco uniform. They would see the problems that employees and customers had at first hand and understand them better, but afterwards they would also report feelings of pride and involvement: they understood how the company made their customers' lives better. A tin of beans is never just a tin of beans.

That emotional connection, remembering why you get up early or work late, is what keeps you going in the bad times. Having fun is not the same thing as having a laugh. For some reason, in my career I seem to have joined many businesses which were having a challenging time. Recently, most of them have been startups with an idea, some of which have lost their way, which quickly extinguishes the enjoyment. But in startups, los-ing enthusiasm for the work is fatal, because often that commitment to succeed is most of what you have at that moment: your startup is an idea looking for a sustainable business model, and the desire to explore and create is the only advantage that you have.

In this tough situation, we are all faced with a choice. We can say: "This is challenging, and that is a scary, negative thing, and so I'm going to give up on it." Or say: "this is challenging, which means I can give this some fresh thought, fresh ideas, take the limitations away, find inspiration and dream about what this situation could lead to."

If you take the first road (which few people would blame you for doing), then there's a problem: you may cut yourself off from many of the things that, in this chapter, we will discover create satisfaction at work. The second road is tougher in the short term, and risky too. But when you are with people alongside you to share the challenge, and when you all realize that you're serious about turning things around, then it becomes a wonderful, inspiring moment. This, for me, is fun.

In those cases, fun can also become infectious. Often I find my biggest challenge after a year is holding onto the coat tails of the people who were beaten down and negative when we made the plan and took the photos of how things used to be. As things begin to change, they try to fly to the moon too fast and leave us all behind, but that's a problem we can all handle.

Not everyone will try to fly. Some people are uncomfortable with change, and don't want to turn their lives upside down. They have responsibilities, kids, and they have already found the work they love to do. This is not a negative in your team, *as long as that is where they find their joy*. At Porsche, for example, as I was trying to create a world of limitless change and possibility, one of the most skilled workers in the company came to me: "Please Kev," one of my regional managers begged, "never promote me."

How could I refuse? He was responsible for a large part of the Porsche customer experience, and everyone admired him and his work. He had found the ultimate pleasure in the job he wanted to do, and few of us are that lucky. "Just leave me doing this, because I love it," he said, "I'm happy."

So, we did. Every business needs people who take pleasure in keeping the machine working while others around them work to rebuild it. People who are not resistant to change, but they're not naturally going to be agents of change either. They're happy, and they make us happy, because they are having fun already. Their contribution gives others the potential to create change.

What is fun?

It might seem that fun is a slippery idea. We have fun when we change, except if we prefer not to change. Fun is achievement, but we can have fun imagining the things we want to achieve.

The point is that fun is the outcome of our process, not something you buy in a tin. It just so happens to be an essential component of creativity and hard work, which makes the process work even better, and so becomes a virtuous circle.

But you can't invent fun at short notice or add it to what you do as an extra ingredient. Some leaders attempt this, for example creating an "optional" team pizza evening, at which fun is compulsory. You can't not attend, even if you spend the time secretly wondering how soon you can go home to see your family. This is backwards: when work is fun, you want to share the good times with the team, which makes work fun. But it starts with the work.

If inspiring leadership is about creating the culture where people feel they can relax and be honest, then it also doesn't feel right to regularly schedule fun in the calendar. If anything, it sends the message that fun and work are distinct activities. We spend much of our waking lives at work: according to the OECD, on average about 40 hours every week. If you're the boss, you can add, on average, another eight hours on to that – or, effectively, another day's work a week. You have one life, and so do your team. You can't schedule fun only for times when you've finished the day job, because you'll have a rotten life.

We therefore need to think carefully about what parts of a job can be fun. In 2016, a think tank called the Happiness Research Institute asked the researchers TNS Gallup to survey 2,500 employees on what made them happy at work. The results[2] are an excellent guide to what leaders need to remember when they want to make work fun.

The report identified eight aspects of what made the people in the survey happy at work:

Purpose We have mentioned this many times already. It is the single most important aspect of inspiring leadership: it connects the vision to the team. It is also a guide to what may be lacking when the team is listless. At Porsche, how can you inspire people with purpose to sell the experience of owning a car which they have never been allowed to drive?

Mastery The feeling of being competent and in control, and being able to perform the tasks we're asking – even if those tasks are very demanding.

Leadership As the leader of your team, they are happier knowing that there is control, organization, and that you listen to them.

Influence Your team are not your slaves, and they are not robots. Employees who feel that what they say and do makes a difference in the team have more fun.

Achievement More of this later: but victories, large and small, create satisfaction.

Work–life balance The feeling that the two aspects of our lives are sustainable. You can ask for extraordinary commitment from your team (and one day, you definitely will), but if you do it every day, you kill the commitment that you nurtured at the outset.

Colleagues Well, it is a team.

Money You might have been thinking about this as you read the other items on the list. Having had very little money growing up, and having had times in business where I was in danger of losing everything, I can agree that some money is better than no money at all.

It solves a lot of problems. At the very least, it allows us to come to work knowing that we have provided for the people we care about, and are not forced to work in jobs we hate just to keep a roof over our heads.

But which of these, do you think, is the most significant determinant of happiness at work?

From the results, we know for sure which the least important one is: money. Salary is not only the least important factor in determining our level of satisfaction, but it also has the least impact in changing the level of our happiness. Simply put: you bribe a sad team to have fun.

Of course, this isn't always true. If one of your team is struggling with debt, or health, and money would ease those worries, that's going to dominate their emotions. But money does not create long-term team happiness at work. There are several reasons for this:

It's not about the money, it's about the comparison Research consistently shows that our happiness when getting more money is mostly based on getting more than the person sitting next to us. If the whole team gets a bonus, this will not move the needle in this respect.

We become accustomed to money quickly A bonus has a short-term effect, and a pay rise soon becomes business as usual. It rarely produces long-term differences in happiness. Incentives do not have to be expensive to have meaning. For example: when I ran Porsche in the UK, we couldn't afford a meaningful cash bonus. Instead, one of the bonuses with the biggest impact that we ever paid to staff were some "Team Porsche" jackets. I secretly found the jacket size of every member of staff in the company, and had them designed and made. You couldn't buy these jackets in a shop. You had to be part of the team to have one, and staff wore them with pride as we continued our journey to success. I still have mine.

Lottery winners are not happier than the rest of us The economist Angus Deaton and the psychologist Daniel Kahneman investigated happiness[3] using data from the Gallup-Healthways Well-Being Index in the US, which asks 1,000 people every day about what is making them satisfied with their lives. They found satisfaction has two components: how we evaluate our whole lives, and how much fun we're having right now. There was a consistent result: happiness rose steadily with earnings until the family earned $75,000 (about £48,000 in the exchange rate at the time). Then it flatlined. We don't keep getting more satisfied with our lives as we get richer, as long as we can earn £48,000.

If money doesn't equal fun at work, what does?

By far the most important elements of having fun in the Happiness Research Institute research were a sense of purpose, our relationships with colleagues and our belief that we are achieving something. And for inspiring fresh motivation, the things that will have the biggest effect are slightly different: giving a team purpose is the most important, but mastery and work–life balance have the other largest effects. Among the people in the survey, half of their motivation is bundled with the first two, and another 20% with the third. As usual, changing their salary has the least effect.

Here are the statements that the most motivated people agreed with: they felt "proud of their job", they "experienced professional satisfaction" through the job, and they "made progress" at work.

Because sense of purpose is so important to inspiring leadership, it's worth looking closely at where this purpose comes from. It's no more common in big or small companies, or teams, but it is slightly different. While the same proportion of people agreed that they had a sense of purpose in startups and multinationals, there are at least two different sources of inspiration. On the one hand, it's possible to feel that you have a sense of purpose because you're part of a big organization that does things that affect millions of people every day. On the other, you can enjoy what you're creating because you meet your customers, or live in the same town as them, and so you see the effect of what you do on the community. All businesses mix the two in different proportions, and all of us have slightly different triggers for enjoyment. Your job as leader is to create the environment that inspires people to find their fun.

How do we create fun?

Purpose, mastery, achievement, colleagues: you could interpret this as the idea that creating fun at work is like making a checklist, with separate ideas for each. In reality it's much more like tuning a car engine. All the components have to work together for the whole thing to function. There are, however, three ways to tune the engine that have a massive impact. By coincidence (or not) they match the three things in the research into happiness that have the biggest impact: purpose, mastery and balance.

Build trust through OVT

Research shows that mutual trust is hard to build. Initially, members of teams may start to trust by doing a mental calculation: on average, do I get more if I trust that person than if I don't trust? This is purely transactional, and it happens when we don't know each other well, we've worked in an atmosphere of backstabbing or broken promises, and we don't communicate. But as we see and hear evidence that honesty and integrity have a high value, we can base their trust on knowledge rather than calculation. It's still a transaction, but it has room to grow.

This is like the trust we place in someone who sells us a shirt on the internet, where our decision to click "buy" is based on our previous purchase or on reading a good review. It is not a creative relationship, but it reduces the stress of working in a team. As the relationships between members of the team deepen, then the trust can become something more profound. For the first time, trust at this level isn't about not having any weaknesses (we all have many), or successfully hiding those weaknesses (as an online shop might try to do). It's about understanding our individual abilities and strengths, and working to make the best of them, while helping to correct weaknesses. This is creative, because we're changing.

The final level of trust is based on instinctively identifying with the team and its vision. We can speak up, and we speak for each other. We share the work, and share the credit. We ask for advice, offer it positively, and listen to feedback. Conflict is constructive, feedback is golden. Things don't have to be perfect to have fun, because you have both a shared purpose and mastery of the situation.

The problem is that, as a leader, you don't have much time to wait for trust to build. You may also have inherited a situation of distrust. This is why OVT – One Version of the Truth – is vital. Until you have that, you can't even get to stage one, because no one can work out whether to trust anyone else or not. OVT is the price of entry, but it isn't creative in itself.

But it can be creative if we use it to build trust, giving us something to commit to. When we communicate more openly, we know what is expected. We believe we will all be heard. Properly done, honest sharing through teamwork is a way to accelerate the trust-building process, which will create a feeling of fun, which inspires motivation, which in turn inspires closer teamwork.

An example of this came from my early months at Fairline, the boat-builder that was on the point of mutiny when I arrived in August 2013. Recall that the company had been trading at a loss for some time, and making its staff redundant. Four weeks after I started, I was already worrying about staff morale, which seemed the dominant problem. I wasn't having fun at that point. I was working from 6am to 11pm, eating bad food, living in a hotel. "Don't let everyone down," I wrote to myself in my note-book, "Keep standing back and looking at the big picture."

The big picture showed that no one else was having fun either. As I wrote that in my notebook, other employees were at home, worried that they would be made redundant, convinced that management had a secret plan to get rid of them, suspicious of the others who might take their job, frustrated that they had good ideas that were lost in the noise. I couldn't change the history, but I wanted us to move forward. Some had given up on trust, both in the factory and among management. All their jobs must have been a living hell. For a company built on three generations of crafts-men, some of their work was beginning to suffer, and some of our custom-ers had noticed. "Staff change creates lack of confidence," I wrote. "Some managers are unsure where to start or how to engage . . . don't lose peo-ple off the back of the group." Too many staff had been programmed to fail, I wrote, and were becoming comfortable with it.

Imagining "fun" in a culture like this is difficult, but I knew that there were plenty of opportunities to build trust, which would create enjoy-ment in time. One simple way: we took the locks off the internal doors. People from the shop floor could come to see the war room, and me if they needed to. But we needed to actively build trust between me and the team members, who had become disconnected from what the com-pany did.

"Breakfast with Kev" was one contribution. We needed to establish a common foundation, based on the truth. We couldn't pretend there were no problems, so just pretending to be happy, or putting a brave face on it, would simply be a different way of avoiding the truth. It's all very well to build a plan, but unless you can engage everybody in that plan, it would be just a piece of paper on a wall. I wanted to invite them to give their ideas, and their perspective, on how to get this to the level where we wanted to be. I walked around the building a lot, I walked around the factory a lot. I spent a lot of time trying to understand the detail, but sometimes I'd get lost in it too. I needed to elevate everybody away from that, and make sure we had a perspective on the big picture.

So every second Thursday, from 8:30am until 10am, we set up breakfast in the boardroom. We purposefully used the boardroom to make it a less exclusive place. There would be croissants and coffee and pastries and fruit, and we would randomly choose eight members of the entire team at any level. Sometimes one of the directors would be there, and other times you'd have a couple of 17-year-old junior apprentices.

There had never been one version of the truth at Fairline, and so naturally the staff took anything I said with a pinch of salt. That blocked the potential for fun, because you can't enjoy the job without trusting your team.

On the other hand, I knew there were potential leaders in there who could help inspire that trust. "Fairline has got talent, find it . . . Looking for leaders at every level," I wrote to myself.

For Breakfast with Kev, the agenda was simple. They'd get an hour and a half to tell me what they thought. We'd have breakfast, sit and we'd talk. We'd just talk. No notes, no paperwork. I'd have a list of their names so I didn't embarrass myself, or them. I invited them to introduce themselves, we would chat a bit about what they'd seen in the business, their history, the potential they saw in the business, what they thought the priorities were.

They could talk back to me, because they could see I was human. Many of them took the opportunity to give me some home truths. A few were angry, and they would take a position and pick an argument. That bit into everyone else's time, which wasn't good. But most of the time I met people who were committed to the job if they were given the chance, who were prepared to give you their opinion, but at the same time were prepared to listen and debate and maybe find a way to negotiate a route towards resolving the big issues that they cared about.

It was also an opportunity to break down barriers. I invited a union shop steward to one of the breakfasts. He had made a point of being confrontational in front of the factory staff each time we held an update meeting. After the breakfast, I invited him to my office for a private discussion about how we could work together more effectively. The meeting was productive, and at the end he admitted: he had never been into the CEO's office before.

"Try my seat for size," I said.

I took a photograph with his camera as he sat in the CEO's chair. Then he shared the photograph with everyone he knew. We put it in the company newsletter, to everyone's amusement. Our relationship improved from that moment, and everyone benefited from that.

Building trust by sharing reduces many of the problems that suck the fun out of what we do. As a leader, it is your job to reverse that process, and create trust based on a shared identity. Be positive, open, honest and transparent. Do not lose people off the back, because we're all in this together. The good news: this is fun, in itself.

Truth is not what leaders decide it is. It is something we share, that we agree on – and when we don't agree, our common sense of purpose inspires us to resolve the difference.

Create many small wins

We've spoken about how 50-day projects can retain momentum. Partly that's because they give us opportunities to celebrate. Every time we make progress, we celebrate it. It doesn't matter if you wave a flag or ring a bell, whatever it is, the message is the same: "We did it."

When we discussed project planning we mentioned the research of Harvard Business School professor Teresa Amabile and her colleague

Stephen Kramer, who researched the value of progress by tracking 12,000 diary entries from 238 individuals, and matching it to a measure of how much fun they were having at work. "Of all the things that can boost emotions, motivation, and perceptions during a workday, the single most important is making progress in meaningful work. And the more frequently people experience that sense of progress, the more likely they are to be creatively productive in the long run," they concluded.[4]

They found that our "inner work life" – effectively the emotions, motivations and perceptions that we have every day – is driven by how positive we feel, which in turn is closely connected to how creative we can be, and how much we achieve.

"People are more creative and productive when their inner work lives are positive – when they feel happy, are intrinsically motivated by the work itself, and have positive perceptions of their colleagues and the organization," they argue, and that is driven by the number of positive emotions they experience more than the depth of those emotions. So giving teams regular things to feel happy about creates a much better sense of fun at work than having one or two massive wins in a year (and both, clearly, create more fun than ruling by fear). Those emotions aren't just satisfaction: the employees in their experiment reported joy, warmth and pride.

"Small but consistent steps forward, shared by many people, can accumulate into excellent execution, progress events that often go unnoticed are critical to the overall performance of organizations," they concluded.

Work as long as it is productive

I get too emotional about my work. I've been in situations that have been very, very stressful, and my default response to that has been to overwork. I spent eight years working in Switzerland driving the growth of Eurotax-Glass's, coming home at weekends. I was away from my wife and young family, working 8am to 11pm for four years of that. I would come home on a Friday night, sleep for much of the weekend, and fly back again at 5.00am on Monday. I can tell you this: it's not healthy, and it's not a good way to lead.

But it's enjoyable when you feel you are achieving something to just keep going, and soon you're demanding that of others. So now I can say, I don't believe in working long hours. I will go round the businesses I work with at 5pm and say to the team, "Go. I'm paid to stay here. You lot, go home."

For me, it's still fine to do this some of the time. These days I'll sit down at 10am in my office, after I finish at the gym. I will get up for a coffee a few times in the day, and finish late at night. But I know what is expected of me and what I have committed to do, and I have control. The OECD[5] asked workers in its member countries whether they were happy about the length of time they allocated to four areas: family, social contact, paid work and hobbies. Fewer than 25% of European workers responded that they felt the amount of time they spent in each of the four areas was right.

That satisfaction makes you want to put in the extra effort that makes a difference. It doesn't necessarily mean putting in long hours. When you are not working, go home, see your family, play football, ride your bike, go to the pub, do whatever you want to do. But in working hours, be really effective and efficient.

Your work is about enjoying the challenge, being in control and producing results. As an inspiring leader, it's your responsibility to provide that balance in your team.

Fun is creative, creativity is fun

We looked at what fun means at work, and found out that all the things an inspiring leader cares about – involvement, commitment, truth, honesty, communication and trust – are the things that generate fun. Fun drives positive thinking and it is this positivity which helps us to make the impossible possible. I try to apply this approach to life in general – never forget that we're only here once, and so in everything I do I try to make it fun. Effort doesn't always have to be focused on a business problem to be worthwhile. Fun is positive simply because it is so much better than the alternative.

In the real world – the one in which we must never forget we operate – fun isn't something you can command, or simply add to a team as if it were a sprinkling of magic dust. It must be part of the leadership style. We called this section "Create", and fun is a very important aspect of that, because it is something that the team creates among themselves. An inspiring leader creates a culture within which the team has fun and is motivated to create the improvements that the business needs.

Notes

1. Ipsos. 2016. Edenred Ipsos Barometer. *edenred.com*.
2. Happiness Research Institute and TNS Gallup. 2016. *Job Satisfaction Index*. Denmark: HRI.
3. Robison, J. 2011. Happiness is love – and $75,000, *Gallup Business Journal*, 17 November.
4. Amabile, T. and Kramer, S. 2011. The power of small wins, *Harvard Business Review*, May.
5. OECD. 2011. *Work and Life Balance*. Paris: OECD Publishing.

Chapter 12

No One Is an "Only a . . ."

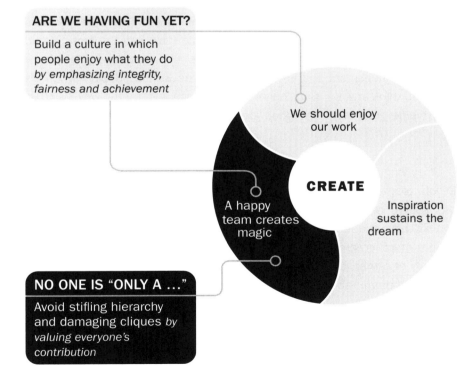

ARE WE HAVING FUN YET?

Build a culture in which people enjoy what they do *by emphasizing integrity, fairness and achievement*

We should enjoy our work

CREATE

A happy team creates magic

Inspiration sustains the dream

NO ONE IS "ONLY A ..."

Avoid stifling hierarchy and damaging cliques *by valuing everyone's contribution*

I f you emphasize that everyone is involved in planning, that the vision belongs to all of us and that trust creates the creative working environment, then you treat everyone with respect. But under pressure it is easy to create hierarchies, to use rank to try to intimidate others.

In this chapter we will look at why it matters that you live with the idea that no one is an "only a . . .". From the cleaner who makes sure that cars don't drip oil, to the bulldozer driver who cuts a runway in the Arctic circle, this book is full of the people who make everyone's success possible by using skill, judgement and hard work. We'll see what's possible when we refuse to think anyone is an "only a . . .", but also understand why we often undervalue great work and good ideas because of where they're coming from.

If, having read this chapter, you become more likely to give someone in your team a chance to surprise you, or put more time into making sure that everyone is valued, and knows it, then my experience suggests that you will have made a big step towards becoming an inspiring leader and have a much greater chance to succeed. Every one of us is somebody's mother, or father, or brother, or sister, or husband, or son, or daughter. We're all human, so show respect to the people who work for you. They want to do a good job, so give them the opportunity to do it by valuing their contribution.

"Somebody like you"

The first pineapple to be raised in England was grown at Dorney Court, just outside Windsor. It was presented to Charles II in 1661. Dorney Court itself was built in 1440. For the thousands of tourists who visit every year, it is the epitome of old English grandeur and privilege: antique furniture, precious objects and a family who have owned the house for four centuries.

When he was 15, Ryan Wasmuth used to cut the grass at my home in Reading, west of London. I paid him £5. I was working at Porsche at the time. He loved cars, and he used to ask how he could get one of the cars that I used to have parked outside the house. I didn't know it then, but he didn't like school much because he is severely dyslexic. Soon after I met him, he left school with a single qualification in art, and set up his own gardening business.

He went from being Ryan and a shovel, to Ryan and a shovel and a van, then Ryan, a shovel, a van and a dog, and then Ryan, a shovel, a van, a dog and a concrete mixer. As he built up his landscaping business, he was still taking care of our garden. "One day," he used to say to me, "I want to own a garden centre."

He didn't have qualifications or capital, but he had a dream that he was committed to. "I want to build Britain's best gardening destination," is what he said and, liking what I heard, I offered to give him advice if he ever had a chance of realizing his dream.

Ryan put me on the spot: "Would you invest in me?" he asked.

And I thought: *yes, I would.*

One day early in 2011, he said to me, "Come and have a look at this," and took me to Dorney Court Kitchen Garden, in the shadow of the great house. It was a garden centre but the previous owners hadn't been able to make a business out of it and the place was a mess. It was a wreck, completely broken, and it wasn't a viable business in its current state. When we did some research we found that there were 110 other garden centres in the area, many on main roads, owned by large firms with plenty to invest. This would be a large step up for him. I knew he was very bright, and a hard worker, but Ryan's dyslexia was so bad that, when he sent me emails, my spell check didn't have any suggestions. I had complete confidence in Ryan's creativity. He was (and is) a wonderful garden designer, but at that point he had no idea about how to run a business like this. When I tried to talk to him about profit, loss, accounts and cashflow, he'd just say, "Yeah, okay."

I'd say, "You haven't got a clue what I'm talking about, have you?" And he admitted that he didn't.

On the other hand, he had found something with a lot of potential. Tourists who visit Windsor Castle also flock to Dorney. It was 400 metres from Eton and Dorney Lake, and we were about to get a million people past the door in 18 months' time, because in 18 months the 2012 Olympic rowing and kayaking events would be held there.

So Ryan took his landscaping business and folded that into Dorney Court Kitchen Garden, and I put some cash in too. He took out a bank loan, and we acquired this failed business. The first thing we did was to make a statement by giving the remaining staff smart uniforms, and invite them to be a part of the plan, the vision for what this garden centre could be. We had 30 days to turn a patch of scrub into a classic English garden. Ryan, and the three people he had asked to work for him, laboured day and night. I joined them, pushing a barrow around, literally helping to build the business by hand.

In two months, we had created one of the most beautiful garden centres in the area, in a 600-year-old walled garden with its own cafe. For the opening Ryan invited people that he had known from childhood, some of the clients from his landscaping business, and the lady of the house agreed to cut the ribbon. On opening day at the beginning of 2011, the sun shone on his hard work, and customers who had abandoned Dorney Court Kitchen Garden years ago returned to see what it had become.

Ryan came over to me. He's 6ft 5in tall, and built like a weightlifter, but he was visibly upset. "Do you see that woman over there?" he said. I did.

"She used to be my teacher. You know what she's just said to me?"

If I'd been her, I would have said: "Well done Ryan, what you and your team have done is inspiring. We clearly didn't see the amazing potential you have as a leader." But she didn't say that.

Ryan said: "She just said to me, 'How does somebody as thick as you do something like this?'"

Our instinct to think "only a . . ."

You've probably known someone who has had a similar experience. It might have happened to you. Our instinct to undervalue or dismiss people who are not obviously like us is a problem that many leaders suffer from.

My role model in how to value a team has always been my dad. When I was growing up, he was the chief engineer of a power station in North Wales. He had served his time as an apprentice and a mechanic. He got his engineering qualifications at night school, and gradually worked his way to the top job.

By the time I was 16 and 17, he could swing me a job as a labourer at the power station in the summer holidays. Labourers would do everything from painting walls to gardening, anything that needed to be done. As the kid, I had another job too: to be the one who was the butt of the jokes. The men I worked with all knew that my dad was the chief engineer, but we all knew that I was in their world now and, though they would have plenty of fun winding me up, they were never aggressive to me. They respected my dad, even though he wasn't one of them anymore, and they told me so.

I asked them why, and they told me: he judged them fairly and valued them for what they contributed. "He treats everyone the same. He is always honest. He is straight with us: if he isn't happy, he'll tell you." That was a lesson for me,

This was in the 1970s. There were labour problems everywhere, regular strikes, but the power station was a strong community, built on mutual respect, pride in the job and the understanding that we supported each other when we worked as a team.

More than 100 years of what came to be called management science have, unfortunately, eroded this principle. It all started with the idea of Taylorism, the ideas created by Frederick Winslow Taylor, the author of *The Principles of Scientific Management*, published in 1899. In the book, Taylor describes how he saved money for his employer, the Bethlehem Steel Company. He noted that, on average, his workers could load only 12.5 tons of pig iron a day into train carriages for transport. He thought this could be improved, so he found 10 of his best workers, and timed them loading bars of pig iron for 14 minutes. He then multiplied this by the hours in the day, moved the target 40% downwards to factor in breaks and rests, and decided that the real target should be 47.5 tons.

He appeared not to notice (or preferred not to notice) that the intensity of a 14-minute test would be unlikely to last for an entire shift. He could not find anyone in the company who could hit the target, and was eventually fired from Bethlehem Steel.

His belief was, however, that working people could never be trusted to work hard without "scientific management". The popularity of this idea with business owners over many years went a long way to creating the them-and-us culture that I think creates dysfunctional teams. In his *Principles*, Taylor explained that, as far as he was concerned, most workers were "only a . . .":

> "The science of handling pig iron is so great and amounts to so much that it is impossible for the man who is best suited to this type of work to understand the principles of this science, or even to work in accordance with these principles, without the aid of a man better educated than he is."

There are two problems here. The first is that he believes it is impossible to trust workers to act in the interests of the company, because they don't understand its value. In the previous chapter, we saw that the reality is the opposite: feelings of being trusted are one of the most important elements of a happy team. In the next chapter, we'll also see how your ability to trust as a leader is one of the most important ways to sustain improvement.

The other problem is that he instinctively believes that "the man best suited" to hard work is unprepared to make decisions and, for decisions to have any positive value, they need to be made by someone with education.

Taylor would probably have considered that these ideas were so obvious that they didn't need an explanation. These sorts of snap judgements – that large numbers of people in our business, or our team, have little to offer – are a leftover of evolutionary biology. *The Atlantic* magazine describes the tendency to discriminate against or ignore everyone that doesn't fit our preconceived ideas of important:

> "Our brains today take in more than 11 million pieces of information at any given moment; because we can process only about 40 of

those consciously, our nonconscious mind takes over, using biases and stereotypes and patterns to filter out the noise."[1]

This is an understandable bias, but it will damage your ability to lead.

As soon as you consider that team members are "only a . . ." you're closing your mind to their contribution, which may be based on their far more detailed (and therefore far more realistic) knowledge of the situation than yours. You are also failing to spot talent because it doesn't fit what you expect it will look like. Finally, you are closing your mind to what you can learn from the people who do the job every day.

For example, I prefer whenever possible to have meetings for everyone in the business, because what happens in the business affects every-one. If you propose this, you might not be popular with senior managers, whose exclusive access to the leader is one of the perks of the job. Keron Hurlstone, who worked with me at EurotaxGlass's, remembers when we introduced all-company meetings.

> "I remember having a meeting, and it didn't matter what role you did at the company, whether you were dispatcher, in telesales, everyone was equal at that point," she says, "I can also remember that it was uncomfortable for some of the managers, who weren't used to this."

At EurotaxGlass's, we operated in 31 countries and we aimed to be inclusive of all levels, but also of all nationalities. This can be just as dis-ruptive if one country considers itself to be the hub of the business, and everywhere else just spokes. We decided to inform and integrate as much as possible, and so one year we even brought the entire company (more than 400 people), at every level, to Zurich. When the teams arrived for a black-tie ball we'd planned during the weekend they were there, we handed them their table assignments. The tables were mixed for all levels and all nationalities.

Good ideas come from everywhere

It's always tempting to try to be the cleverest person in the room. If you really are always the cleverest person, you should hire some better staff. Or, more likely, look harder for the genius ideas that you are missing.

At Fairline, I was certainly not the smartest person when it came to boats. When the team realized that we would act on their ideas, there were so many suggestions that we had to put whiteboards at the end of each of the production lines. We invited the staff, every time they had a bright idea, to put it on the whiteboard. Then we trusted them to implement the good ideas in the business.

One day, a young member of the staff in his mid 20s came to us. Every boat we made was a one-off, and so each boat was fitted slightly differently according to the client specification and the approach of the team building it. This meant that each boat had slightly different pipework that snaked about the hull, and was hard to fix if there was a problem. He had a better idea: lay a central spine of standard pipework down the boat with spurs off to all the points where you needed water. We quickly saw it was far more efficient, and we immediately implemented it.

I don't give prizes for suggestions: I believe that they are part of the job. But our production director came to me and said: "This change has had quite a significant impact, we want to reward him."

They talked to him. He had a young family, and he wanted to study at night school, but couldn't afford it. So we paid for him to study in the evening for a qualification that would help his career. He had been a hero for us, and it was good to help him to be a hero for his family.

When the team believed in the future, they started to question everything, and answer those questions using their own initiative. We were dealing with customers who spend £5 million on a boat, but when they came to visit us, in the middle of nowhere, one of the staff would borrow a manager's car and go to the airport and pick them up. When they got to our office, they waited in reception.

So I recruited two more people who turned out to be at least 5% genius to redesign the front office. One of them had worked for a concierge company, the other in first class for a major airline. We told them to introduce a world-class level of service. They came up with a list of things to do and things to change, and they transformed the front of house. Thanks to them we started to completely reimagine how we treated our customers. We made plans to greet the customers at the airport, and put them in a helicopter, so they could fly to see their boat. This wasn't about spending money, because most of the improvements we made cost nothing. The rest, the clients would happily pay for.

When people feel like heroes at their work, they want to show that to the people they care about. One year into our recovery, we decided we'd have a family open day. Part of my work involves speaking at major conferences. I had earned some speaking fees talking to other companies about our remarkable turnaround, and I donated them so we could hire a marquee, have a barbecue and stage a battle of the bands (many of the boat-builders, it turned out, were excellent musicians). The lads were so proud of what they'd built that, by the day before, they had decided to put story walls up around the factory, to show their families how they built the boats. It was an extraordinary day which built pride and confidence.

Feedback is golden

Someone has to be in charge. As the leader, this is you. But the only way you become an inspiring leader is to be open and to accept criticism from the people who work in your team. The natural instinct of many leaders is to bite or react, but honest communication between levels in your team is a gift. Feedback is golden, so seek it out and use it wisely.

When you are criticized, the best instinct is to keep your mouth shut until you have thought about it. Recognize that you're not omnipotent, you're just the leader of this team, at this moment. Today, you just happen to be in a different position to other people.

This is fundamental because it is the best way to reinforce one of the most important principles in inspiring leadership: OVT, one version of the truth. The idea is not that this is a truth you create and impose on others: it doesn't matter what they experience, because they are only the people who do the job. The authenticity of their experience may not be what you want to hear, but it is the truth, and the truth has the same value, no matter whose mouth it comes from.

There are several ways to seek out this truth from people who work below you in the hierarchy. One of the best, I have found, is simply to be visible. I've known of bosses who come in, go into their office, close the door, stay in there all day, and go home at night, without speaking to anyone below their direct reports. You're not just there to manage numbers. You're there to inspire a team, and how do you inspire them if you don't communicate with them?

Personally, I go out of my way to walk the business. Go out of my way to take bits of paper to people and put them in their hand, rather than emailing them. A lot of the time it's just an excuse to sit down with somebody and start a conversation, not always about the business.

Also, we often have our management meetings standing in front of our ideas wall, and we will share those ideas and discuss them. You have an idea, and you are part of the conversation. The alternative is that your bright idea goes up to the Head Office, you don't hear anything, and then maybe nothing happens. Or, if it does, no one bothers to talk to you about it. This sends the message that, even if your idea is good, you're only the person who had the idea, and so you don't matter.

The third is to take some time to brief people properly. Don't micro-manage, but do explain why projects exist. I've never met anybody that wants to do a bad job, but I've met a lot of people who are doing a bad job because they don't know what's expected of them. Too many businesses and too many leaders just dive into the job, thinking that this is energetic and motivational. Everyone starts running, but they're not quite sure which way they're running. Truth is a casualty, not because anyone has lied, but because everyone's got different information. You just get a hairball.

Don't rely on positional authority. Your authority comes from the fact that what you're doing is the best idea, that we all agreed it was the best idea, and that everyone is committed to it. Acting the boss does not mean telling people what to do. It also does not mean leaning on anyone else's positional authority ("the board thinks that we should . . ."). If you are going to lead it, the decision belongs to you, even if it was made some-where else.

Next, don't be afraid to deliver difficult news. Recently I was coaching a company that was aiming for world-class standards of execution. They had been out for a social evening the night before, and when we started, I wrote the numbers 8, 4 and 2 on the board. What was this? 8:42? It was the time we started to work, compared to the scheduled 8am start. Being world class has its own schedule, which doesn't get put back for hango-vers. Therefore, respect for the team is to also tell them, directly and honestly, when performance falls short. This works both ways. If the least senior members of the team do their job, and managers are lazy, late, or even just don't bother to acknowledge their contribution, this devalues the work that has been done. It is your job to spot this early, and talk about it. No one has more or less responsibility to the team because of their job title or status.

Getting paid

In 2015, the consultancy Manifest calculated that the average chief executive in the UK was paid £4.3 million.[2] Even allowing for inflation, senior executive pay has tripled since 1998. Average pay, during this time, rose by 12% in real terms.[3] Pensions and Investment Research Consultants, a specialist in how companies are governed, calculates that the average FTSE CEO earns 130 times the average salary of employees. In 1998, the multiple was 47 times.

While, in my experience, many of the people earning exceptional salaries are also working exceptionally hard, and have exceptional skills, there comes a point at which their rewards are not good for the team.

We all want to do the best for ourselves and our families, but when the pay and conditions that leaders experience are in a different league to those that the rest of the team gets, they can't help but feel the hierarchy. In 1992, when I was running Porsche in the UK, the new group CEO, Wendelin Wiedeking, agreed to pledge some of his private assets to help secure credit for the company, which at that time was close to running out of cash. In return, he was granted a 1% share of Porsche profits, which quickly became huge. By 2007–2008 he earned €2 million as a base salary, but an additional €98 million in profit share.[4] The profit share was in his contract, and so he was entitled to it. But it certainly caused resentment among others in the company.

My approach now has been to focus on creating shared value, especially for my turnaround businesses. If I do well, it's only because I have helped the business to grow. My interests, and the interests of the people who work in the team, are aligned. For the type of company I work for now, I ask for equity, usually between 5% and 20% of the business. I take no salary for the first year, and the second year they pay me as if I were a non-executive director. If I don't stay for three years (or if they decide to kick me out after one or two years), I'll give back a third or two-thirds of the equity.

It's both a motivator to the team, who know I have almost no guaranteed pay, and a motivator for me. I don't need a huge income, but I do need to live.

The team knows that my vision of success is the same as theirs: a profitable company and a secure future. So, to align our incentives, I also create an equity pool for the entire staff. If the business is successful, they all share in the value they created. Why not? They made the success possible.

The hidden value of knowhow

My first job was as a civil engineer working on construction sites. When you put up a steel-frame building, the essential job is to "cast the slab", which means you pour hundreds of cubic metres of concrete, with bolts carefully set into it, into the ground. Much of the work in construction is in the foundations.

But when you finish pouring this giant slab of concrete, somebody's got to brush it off. As a 21-year-old I used to wonder why the same people did the job. It couldn't be that difficult. So they gave me a broom, and invited me to have a go. Before I knew it, I was choking with the dust. Everyone was watching me, laughing.

So, for the first time I watched them properly when they brushed a concrete slab. They brought two bags of sawdust. They put just the right amount of water in it to wet it, and they scattered it, and the wet sawdust stopped the concrete dust.

Every job has skills like that: skills that are learned, passed on, not obvious but essential to success. If you forget the contribution that everyone makes, or the person with the skill is disconnected from the project, the job doesn't get done. Whether we are walking to the North Pole, creating a garden, beating panels or serving in a hotel, there are a thousand tasks that must be done well. External exhortations to do the job well aren't enough. The feeling of pride has to come from inside, and that comes when the team values all the work, not just the work people can easily see.

Dr Martin Luther King had an opinion on exactly this subject: if someone is called to be a street sweeper, he said, "He should sweep streets so well that all the hosts of heaven and earth will pause to say, 'Here lived a great street sweeper who did his job well' . . . No work is insignificant. All labour that uplifts humanity has dignity and importance and should be undertaken with painstaking excellence."

At Dorney Court Kitchen Garden, Ryan's excellence has been well rewarded, because he took his strength, his knowhow, and he built on it. As I was writing this book, he has just sold a thriving business to a larger company that can take it to the next stage. In six years, he took Dorney Court from a wreck to becoming one of the top 25 garden centres in the country. It is beautiful. At the age of 40, he has a new dream: to win a gold medal at the Chelsea Flower Show, He's just created a garden that cost £1.5 million, a project that would be too complex for most landscaping businesses to manage.

In the early years, we worked together on the accounts and planning that he never thought he would be able to do. Now he'll quote the numbers back at me. His teachers never found out, but his brain was never the problem. He is very bright. While we're discussing a problem, he's so fast at finding the solution that he's got the answer before most of us have thought through the problem. He now speaks at schools to inspire the next generation, and describes himself to them as "gifted with dyslexia", helping these students to dream about what is possible if they have their own vision of success.

He's also become not just a great gardener, which he always was, but a smart entrepreneur. Not everyone can take this step, but he has discovered, along the way, that he's a natural leader. He knew that to keep growing the garden centre it would take years of hard work for very little return. So he has chosen to focus his work (and capital) into his landscaping business rather than hiring staff for the cafe or working out how to attract more traffic to a garden centre. He has a new vision of success and he's fully committed to it. He's an inspiring leader for his team, who love working for him. No one pulls the wool over his eyes because he's six foot five and knows the job inside out as he's been doing the hard work since he was a teenager. As I write this book he has just built his first garden, on behalf of the BBC, at the RHS Chelsea Flower Show and is about to build his next 1,000-day plan to achieve another level of extraordinary success.

His painstaking excellence built something extraordinary. When he arrives to meet his clients in his new Land Rover Discovery, dressed smartly and managing his team, he's not the Ryan whose teachers gave up on him, and who used to mow my grass for £5 anymore. He's a successful serial entrepreneur, who created his opportunity through vision and hard work.

Which is a lesson to Ryan's former teacher, who needs to learn how to inspire.

Everyone in the team matters

When I'm looking for people to employ, I'm always on the hunt for people who are adaptable. Lindy at Conceptual Eyes calls this adaptability "three up, three down". It means that the most capable people in your team will be able to communicate with others in the business three levels above, and three levels below. As a leader, you should not only be making sure that you can communicate with people at every level, but that you *do* communicate with them.

For Lindy, this takes her to some unusual locations. Recently she was involved with a mining company merger in South Africa. While we think of business transactions like this as boardroom negotiations, they have huge consequences for everyone in the company. Often those at the top may make assumptions about the people in their teams without ever communicating directly with them.

Lindy's job was to help the mining company give a voice to everyone in the business to discuss the best way forward for the company. This wasn't just about running workshops – it also included spending eight hours underground in a mine. There has been a tangible result: mines that might have been scheduled for closure have been kept open. "A lot of the workforce don't have good English, and so their communication skills in the business are limited," she says about the project, "A company will bring together different cultures and communities, and it's vital that they communicate."

Also, everyone needs to know that their work has value, and it is your job to demonstrate that value to them. At Porsche, I would hand-write a personalized Christmas card to every member of staff with a note about what they had done this year, thanking them for their efforts and ideally making a reference to something I knew they were interested in (sport, music, Formula 1, and so on). This process started in early November, because it took me that long to get them all done. But it had a huge effect on creating a tight bond in the team.

Every day as a leader, whether I think about it or not, I rely on everyone in the team to work well, to use their full creative and technical knowledge, to achieve results that I couldn't achieve on my own. They are the ones who know how to build a boat, or make a better car, or write software. My job has been to make sure that we do that cohesively, collectively and creatively as a team. If you are to achieve something extraordinary, everyone matters.

Notes

1. Mundy, L. 2017. Why is Silicon Valley so awful to women? *The Atlantic*, 1 April.
2. Jenkins, P. 2017. How paying chief executives less can help corporate performance, *Financial Times*, 13 February.
3. Even by 1998 standards, I wasn't earning as much as my peers. My salary at BMW was £150,000 a year. My biggest ever bonus was about £50,000. If my pay packet had been in the millions, I'd have considered myself dramatically overpaid.
4. Autobild. 2015. *Wiedeking verdiente* über *100 Millionen*.

Chapter 13

Catch In, Don't Catch Out

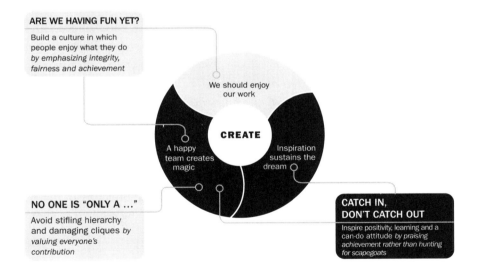

ARE WE HAVING FUN YET?
Build a culture in which people enjoy what they do *by emphasizing integrity, fairness and achievement*

We should enjoy our work

CREATE

A happy team creates magic

Inspiration sustains the dream

NO ONE IS "ONLY A …"
Avoid stifling hierarchy and damaging cliques *by valuing everyone's contribution*

CATCH IN, DON'T CATCH OUT
Inspire positivity, learning and a can-do attitude *by praising achievement rather than hunting for scapegoats*

Many of the good ideas that my teams have profited from have started as bad ideas. If we want to inspire our team to try to do the impossible, there will be mistakes and failures along the way. As a leader, you will have to take failure and create something useful from it.

I never compromise on our shared vision of what we can achieve, but I don't expect perfection. Mistakes are important because they tell us what we will need to change. The message that we're great has no meaning without mistakes. People are not computer programs, and creativity isn't something that you order up when you need it. Trying something means that you will get errors with the trials, and so how you deal with mistakes is vital. I maintain that no one goes through life wanting to do a bad job. But we often deal with mistakes as if they were a betrayal. When we catch out a team member, single them out for criticism or humiliation, we begin to break up the group. Also, we demonstrate the consequences of failure to others, making it less likely that they will try something new, or suggest something interesting.

This chapter is about why I think "catching in" is an important creative force, and how to make sure you lead a team in which mistakes and challenges make you stronger, not weaker. After reading it, I hope you are inspired to look at how you deal with errors and setbacks personally, and in your team. No one is perfect.

Blame culture undermines the team

The joke is that the leader calls a meeting, and announces: "We have a blame culture in this company, and I demand to know who's responsible!"

Blame culture grows naturally if it is not checked, but it will undermine the creativity of your team. In 2014, Ursula Rami and Caroline Gould, two sociologists based in Austria, researched blame culture,[1] which in their words is "characterised by the fact that identifying the person to blame is more important than identifying the cause of the error".

They asked employees of three manufacturing firms to fill in questionnaires about the ways they dealt with mistakes, and what made them admit or cover up their errors. Not surprisingly, many of the workers didn't like owning up to mistakes because of the fear they would be singled out. Three in five thought that admitting to your mistakes was "disadvantageous" to your job, and more than half agreed that, if no one had noticed, why mention your mistakes? When there was bad news to deliver, workers relied on their families the most for support, and slightly less on their colleagues – but only 37% thought that could rely strongly on their supervisors for support.

Getting rid of a blame culture, the authors conclude, is "a transition from a superficial, reactive culture of blame, toward a systems analysis, proactive safety culture . . . the handling of errors should be without prejudices". In other words, unless you can inspire your team to own up to mistakes and failures and discuss them, no one can learn from them.

The researchers found that there were three dimensions to the "catching in" culture that you need to create. The first is for the leader to convince the team that covering up errors is a bad thing. The second is for the leaders not to react to open communication by assigning blame, but to create a culture of learning from mistakes. And the last is to have a culture of support for people and teams who fail, because failure can be just as creative as success. We'll deal with each in turn.

No cover-ups

In the war room, every one of our projects has its own folder, and every folder has traffic-light RAG status, depending on how it's going. I can get a feel for how our 1,000-day plan is working simply by walking around the room and looking at what's on the wall. If, however, I see green all the way around, I'm more disappointed than delighted.

The first reason might be that we're simply going too slowly (see Chapter 10 for more about that). On the other hand, there might be a bigger problem: everything is not OK, and no one wants to be the messenger, because they fear they will be shot.

You need to know how to catch in because you need to hear all the ideas and problems. The feedback that everything is fine may feel positive, but it will give you a false sense of security. As Sir John Harvey-Jones once said: "If you are doing things the same way as two years ago, you are almost certainly doing them wrong."

When Alan Mulally joined Ford Motor Company as its CEO in 2006, the company was on a precipice. Soon it would drive off that precipice, reporting losses of $12.7 billion that year, and losing millions of customers to its rivals along the way. In 2006, Ford lost $5.8 billion in the fourth quarter alone. It had problems in manufacturing, problems in customer relations, problems in strategy, problems in finance. It had a famously poisonous executive culture, with the heads of its different business units competing with each other as much as with its rivals.

The company was forced to pledge nearly all of its US-based assets, from its factories to its logo, as collateral to borrow more than

$23 billion in order to keep investment going while it tried to turn the business around.

Mulally's motto for reinventing the company would be "One Ford". But for that to happen, executives had to learn how to be self-critical, even if it made them vulnerable in front of each other.

Soon after he took over, Mulally called senior executives together to hear reports on how well their business units were performing.[2] They demonstrated performance using colour-coded charts, which were nearly all green, with a little yellow. Only one executive showed a chart with a red box, which was going to delay the launch of a new product range. By the previous standards at Ford, it was a serious mistake.

The room was silent, expecting the under-pressure CEO to chew out the only leader in the group with a failure. Instead, Mulally applauded him.

Mark Fields, who at that time was running Ford in the US, was the only one who had the guts to admit to the depths of the problems in the business.

Mulally had already questioned why, if the company was losing billions of dollars a year, were his direct reports showing him so many green boxes? Mulally remembers what he said: "Mark, that is great visibility and I am glad you understand that. Is there any help you need? Other resources you could get from technical or product development?"

At the moment, most people would have caught Fields out, he caught him in. That moment is now considered a turning point in Ford's culture, in which managers could work together, admit the scale of the problem and begin to dig themselves out of it. Fields took charge of a turnaround plan that meant thousands of redundancies (40% of white-collar workers at Ford in the US lost their jobs) and closures. But Ford was the only one of the big US carmakers that didn't need a government bailout. Its management culture was transformed, and the US became its most profitable business unit. In 2014, Fields succeeded Mulally as CEO.

Ford's road back to profitability began when it stopped covering up bad news.

Encourage communication

Operationally, it's best if you can spot failure as early as possible and not be afraid to confront it. But fear of being caught out leads all of us to misreport, sugar coat, or hide the truth, as happened at Ford. In teams that I lead, I try to set the tone and focus on the issue, not the person, so we try to understand what's going wrong together. Because when we do that, we can learn from each other, and we can stop making the same mistakes over and over.

Communication is a continuum, not a pyramid with a leader at the top. At the lowest levels, everyone has a manager. Those managers have managers who report to the board, and if I am CEO or chairman, they report to me. It doesn't stop there, though. I have to report to investors, shareholders, suppliers, the press or – most importantly – our customers. The information that you transfer to those other parties needs to be accurate, consistent and delivered on time. Sitting on bad news and hoping that it will magically change only makes it worse. If you're going to eat a frog, it's better not to stare at it for too long.

So when someone, anywhere in the team, feels the need to sugar coat the truth, that's very dangerous. Someone else will have to account for that sugar coating at some point, and I have found that the pain of the adjustment is usually greater than if no one had told the white lie in the first place.

In my companies, I spend an hour with each of my immediate team, one on one, every week. The rule: be honest. We are all sometimes reluctant to appear incompetent in front of our colleagues, but there should be no excuse for not being honest in private. The message from me is that we're in the same team. If you're having a tough time, I say, tell me and we will work on it together. We never part with me saying: "It's your mess, you sort it out."

Scapegoating, however, is the default in many business situations. I get angry too when something fails, and it's often hard not to make that personal. But there's a choice: you can either accept that some failure is inevitable and try to learn from it, or go looking for someone to blame (maybe to take the heat off yourself), and lose the chance to improve along the way – not least because everyone will be working as hard as possible to try to convince you it wasn't their fault, or it was nothing to do with them. It is hard to commit to the unknown if you feel you're going to be a scapegoat later.

Amy Edmondson, a professor at Harvard Business School, has spent 20 years talking to businesses about how they deal with the problem of failure. Businesses are generally poor at processing failure, she points out,[3] even when they really want to use failure constructively.

One of the reasons is that we think of failure as one thing, when in reality there are many types. She categorizes the different types of failure, from those that are blameworthy (for example, someone in your team breaks the rules on purpose, or doesn't give the attention that a job needs) to those that are no one's fault, and are arguably "good" failures. In this latter category, we can put the fact that your team were experimenting with a new idea as part of a project, or just had no information about whether it would succeed, but tried it anyway to find out.

In the middle of this scale, there are failures for which someone could possibly be blamed, but for which it is usually better to solve the underlying problem first: for example, the process broke down because it wasn't the right way to approach the task, or the task that the team took on was too difficult to do well, given their skills and training.

"When I ask executives to consider this spectrum and then to estimate how many of the failures in their organisations are truly blameworthy, their answers are usually in single digits – perhaps 2% to 5%," she writes. "But when I ask how many are *treated* as blameworthy, they say (after a pause or a laugh) 70% to 90%."

The result of the personalization of blame, she says, is that the chance to learn, or change, or avoid it next time, is lost. For example, if the team lacks training in an important area of the business, that's a problem you can easily fix. But it is also a problem they might not feel comfortable admitting to their boss.

One other way in which our processes can become a problem is the habit of insisting on measuring success using only changes to key performance indicators (KPIs), even though you're still experimenting on exactly how to change, and where that change is taking the business. If you're truly going to experiment, to push the boundaries and explore what's possible, don't start by giving yourself a set of numbers to achieve. By their nature, they will limit your team's ability to improvise or have new ideas. They may also turn a "good" failure (one that maybe shows you that you really should be rethinking this part of the business) into a "bad" one (one that shows you you're just not hitting a target, even if it's the wrong target).

It is right to ask for openness about failure, but as a leader you need to see the bigger picture and use it constructively, not get lost in the details.

Social support

You also need to create a shared culture in which failure isn't poisonous. Our attitude to failure, if we are not careful, is only going to increase the team's fear of change. Fear of failure also keeps us locked into zombie plans that were exciting once, but are now part of the 3% culture – successful to a limited extent, but getting in the way of our dreams. If you can collectively be open enough to spot failure and act on it, it is extremely creative for the team.

Google's parent company, Alphabet, has a subsidiary called X. It's the research laboratory, and the person in charge is a British entrepreneur called Astro Teller. It has a category of projects it calls "moonshots". It describes them like this: "moonshots live in the grey area between audacious projects and pure science fiction". Instead of 10% gains, they aim for 10x improvements in areas like driverless cars or artificial intelligence.

It also has a very unusual culture about failure: it uses open communication to evaluate all its projects as early as possible. Teams are expected to be direct and honest about the prospects of success. And then, if that leads to failure, they have a party. It celebrates the ambition, and what the team learned, and the fact that, instead of being trapped inside a failing project for years, it can move on to do something else with a better chance of success (at Google, there is always another idea in the birdcage).[4]

It's easy to confuse this type of social support with a culture in which "everything is good", whether it succeeds or fails in the business. Remember you are not praising every idea, you are praising the hard work that was done, and creativity of the idea. Team support does not mean pretending that everything is fine, like the managers at Ford, when it is not. Success only has a meaning because failure exists, and is recognized for what it is.

An example would be my earliest days at Porsche. To change the culture, we had opened the doors to ideas, literally. Instead of locked areas which needed a key card, we let anyone walk around the building. "And my mind is open," I said to staff who took to bringing me their bright ideas in the office, "Talk to me about anything."

There were ideas for everything. Once we had turned on the idea tap, it couldn't be turned off. But not all the ideas were good, not all the considerable energy that was being expended on changing everything was helping us get back to profitability, and we ran the risk of wasting time on bad ideas which squeezed out good ideas. The biggest issue we faced was still the hundreds of unsold cars sitting in stock. So I placed a Post-It note on my new fancy office door. It said: DISC?

It was a reminder to everyone. It stood for: "Does it sell cars?" If whatever they were doing didn't sell cars, we could agree to stop doing it, or considering it, for a time, while we sold our stock. Then, perhaps, we'd get to it. It gave us a simple yardstick with which to approve good ideas, and quickly shoot down the ideas that weren't right, without it getting personal.

I was helped because I was surrounded by colleagues who had the strength and the confidence to point out bad choices without judging them, and to abide by the team's decision and move on.

Social support has another advantage. It allows you to recognize each individual's strengths and build on them, without worrying so much about addressing their weaknesses. In the long term, yes – but for now, let's focus on the strengths and make them stronger.

Each person in the team, if they are supported, doesn't have to be everything. This frees them to be really good at what they are good at. I spend a lot of time saying to people: you're fantastic at this but not this. So how are we going to compensate for that? What is it you need?

An engine of improvement

Your biggest problem should not be finding out who's to blame, it should be the fear of the opportunities that you never discovered, because your team were scared to be wrong.

If the business is stagnating or failing, we learn to live with fear. It nags at us. It's there in the morning, and we take it home with us at night. We rationalize the fear. It can't get worse than it is, can it? Well actually, it can. Once a business is in decline, and it does nothing, the rate of decline can only accelerate.

On the other hand, we have seen in this chapter how it is possible to fail together and learn from it, provided we build structure and processes to tell the truth, to communicate and support each other. We have also seen that this might be an advantage if we want to accelerate the pace of change. Mark Zuckerberg, the CEO of Facebook, explained one of the company's mottos in his letter to shareholders in 2012:[5]

"Moving fast enables us to build more things and learn faster. However, as most companies grow, they slow down too much be-cause they're more afraid of making mistakes than they are of losing opportunities by moving too slowly. We have a saying: 'Move fast and break things.' The idea is that if you never break anything, you're probably not moving fast enough."

Notes

1. Rami, U. and Gould, C. 2016. From a "culture of blame" to an encouraged "learning from failure culture", *Business Perspectives and Research*, 4(2): 161–168.
2. Muller, J. 2014. How Mark Fields overcame doubters to earn the job as Ford's next CEO, *Forbes*, 1 May.
3. Edmondson, A. 2011. Strategies for learning from failure, *Harvard Business Review* (July–August).
4. Remember the birdcage is the place, during planning, where we put the ideas that aren't ready to fly yet.
5. Zuckerberg, M. 2012. Letter to shareholders, *Financial Times*, 2 February.

Chapter 14

Sustaining Success

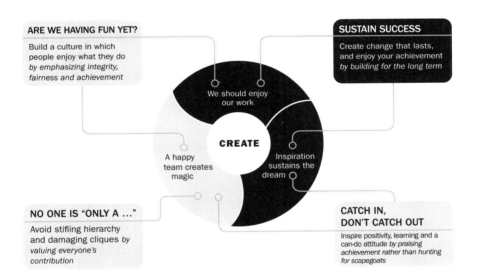

ARE WE HAVING FUN YET?
Build a culture in which people enjoy what they do *by emphasizing integrity, fairness and achievement*

SUSTAIN SUCCESS
Create change that lasts, and enjoy your achievement *by building for the long term*

We should enjoy our work

CREATE

A happy team creates magic

Inspiration sustains the dream

NO ONE IS "ONLY A …"
Avoid stifling hierarchy and damaging cliques *by valuing everyone's contribution*

CATCH IN, DON'T CATCH OUT
Inspire positivity, learning and a can-do attitude *by praising achievement rather than hunting for scapegoats*

With inspirational leadership, you are not just doing something, you are helping to build something. That thing you build needs to stand on its own.

But you are only the leader, and often only for a short time. The bigger job, that will create sustained, deep change, is to give away authority and accountability, in particular authority. As near as possible, you should try to make yourself redundant. You must aim to create a team that knows what it is doing, an engine of change and improvement that can follow the process without you.

So the final part of the section on creativity is about combating the threats to doing this. Too many of the teams I have been involved with have not sustained the improvements they made, and I blame myself for some of that. At Fairline, for example, after the team had worked so hard to get the business back into profit, it was painful to watch new owners adopt a different strategy, which I thought would fail. I told them so, and they dismissed me for expressing this point of view. They followed their chosen path, and the business failed. A lot of committed, hard-working, skilful people lost their jobs as a result. But often I also take great pride in seeing people I have worked with become the leader, and take the business further than I could, into areas I never dreamed of.

To me, sustaining success means helping as many of the next generation of leaders as possible to create their own inspiring successes, and hopefully inspiring others to do the same. That's why I spend so much of my time these days speaking, coaching and mentoring, and it's the reason I wrote this book.

You may be at the beginning of your leadership journey, or maybe you are frustrated by the results you are getting and want to make a change. Or you're doing well, but feel there should be more meaning and satisfaction in what you do: you don't want to just deliver profits once a quarter, your vision is about changing lives. For all of those challenges, it's not just what you do on Monday, but what your team will continue to do every Monday, long into the future. That's what this chapter is about.

Learning to let go

In Chapter 1 I wrote about how, out of 18 companies that the bestseller *Built to Last* identified as having the tools to survive in the long term, seven experienced some form of crisis in the next 10 years, and that 75% of the S&P 500 will change in the next 15 years. In Chapter 5 we discussed the principle of creative destruction: a world in which innovators are essential because they create new, different ways to do the same thing that are much better. The people who dare to think differently suddenly grab a part of the market because their products are cheaper, better or easier to use.

This is the same problem, looked at in two different ways. The negative view is that you are never too big, too successful or too good at what you do to be invulnerable. But, more importantly, it is the same inspiring opportunity: if your vision is more ambitious and the quality of what you create is better, you can do extraordinary things, even if your competition is bigger, richer or more successful.

Chapter 5 was all about how fear holds us back. If you conquer your fear of making hard decisions, you may still be afraid to give others the opportunity to use their own creativity, values and principles to make decisions.

That's a challenging thing to do. But recall from Chapter 11 that the feeling of being trusted inspires people to be happy in their work. After more than a quarter century as a leader, I believe that people naturally want to do a good job, so trust them. My default position is not that people in my teams should earn trust, it's that we should share trust.

There are two practical reasons for this. First, how, in the normal working day, when you want to change and move quickly, can people "earn" trust? There simply isn't time. Second, as I have said: the team knows more about running the business than I do.

This is especially true as businesses become more specialized, or more technology-driven. When I was CEO of Fairline, I didn't know anything about building boats, but I knew how to run a boat-building company. Today I'm involved with a business that sells FinTech technology, I don't know how to code. I don't know anything about broadband technology, but I am helping a broadband company reach new markets and grow. I ask them to place trust in me, and I should do the same in return if we are going to create something that's extraordinary.

Trust alone, however, cannot sustain success. With training, communication and the evidence of results, you can build an instinct for what's good. There are, nevertheless, destabilizing problems all around you. Some of these problems are personal, some of them are organizational, some are political and most have elements of all three. I've picked out five threats to sustaining success, and suggested some ways you can try to mitigate the problems they present. They are:

A new broom Your successor actively tries to be different for its own sake, and the processes you put in place are not strong enough.

Energy vampires and doubters If people are determined not to follow the team's path, they need to be constructively removed from the business.

Events You cannot protect the future so review your plans constantly.

Impatience Profound change may take years. If you try to rush it or cash in, you might destroy all the progress you created.

Hanging on too long Don't overstay your welcome. You know when it is time to move on.

A new broom

Teams and businesses are not democracies. You can build the structures and processes, and you can position the company so that it's performing well, has a strong cashflow and its sales are doing well. Somebody has to continue that. I've seen succession go wrong many times, probably more often than I've seen continuity done correctly.

At Porsche, my colleague Adrian Hallmark had been my right-hand man. He and I shared a lot of values and philosophies, and so he carried on and was very successful. Of course, he an excellent leader who put his own stamp on the role but he built on the foundations we had established. Later, when I left BMW, my successor turned out to be the director who had come to me at the beginning, and who had told me that he had wanted my job, and therefore wouldn't work with me. He went to an overseas division, returned to run BMW GB after I resigned, and, despite the obvious visible signs of success, unpicked a lot of what I had done. It wasn't personal, but we didn't think the same way about how to run a team, and never will.

Often, the problem arises because the owners of the business, or the team, look for an outsider – the so-called "new broom syndrome". The *Harvard Business Review* in 2007 found that about half of large US companies would get a new CEO within four years, and when a new chief executive arrived from outside the company there would be a 25% turnover of executives. When a new boss was appointed from within, there was 17% turnover.[1] This was bad for the team too: of the leaders, only 32% went to jobs that were better, or the same. The rest ended up in worse jobs, or worse teams.

If the team is failing, or has lost momentum, then there's a much stronger argument for a new broom: the research also found that a high-performing team would be much more likely to get a new leader from inside, rather than someone parachuted in from a competitor. That's one reason why it's important to stay in command and out of control (Chapter 9) and keep refreshing what you do. When you leave, move to a new project or get promoted – the rest of your team is more likely to stay intact.

But, when you're working as fast as possible, it's easy to neglect the job of creating leaders. I realize now that, in my career, I haven't given nearly enough time to training our young leaders. I haven't used enough formal training in the businesses I've been involved in, although I have tried to coach people on an individual basis. That's why, with hindsight, I think one of a leader's most important responsibilities isn't to inspire followers. Give yourself a project to create a successor who is ready to step in.

Energy vampires and doubters

Don't waste your time with people who waste your time.

We mentioned the energy vampires in Chapter 4: very few people are so destructive to what you are trying to do that they will also destroy the team. But when you find them, there is no other way to deal with them but to exclude them from what you are doing.

While I criticize the reflex to always look for a new broom, I have to admit that I have often been that broom. Many times when I joined a company I have been viewed with suspicion, even hostility, because people assumed I would impose change. A key part of being an inspiring leader is that you absorb what's going on around you, and you learn from it, and you assimilate the information you need to predict potential outcomes. If you listen well, not only do you earn the right to make changes, but you can head off negativity before it becomes a serious problem.

How you deal with these problems depends on your personality. No single person leads with every one of the skills and attributes that we have discussed. Personally, I'm emotional, sometimes too emotional. I find it very difficult to be cold and hard. I care passionately and always seek to find the best in people – even people who may initially be negative. I really don't like to fire people – and have actually dismissed very few in my time as a leader – but, if you leave destructive person- alities in the team, as soon as you give away authority, they are likely to assert their authority to undermine everything you have achieved together.

Early in my career, I really wanted to be liked – it was important to me to be friendly with people. Now not so much. The reality of the 1,000-day plan has shortened my timetable. Now I show people respect, and I expect respect in return. But as an inspiring leader you must set the tone and the expectations for honest professional communication.

At BMW I heard that the staff nicknamed me the "smiling assassin". To be fair, there were several people who were there when I arrived who should have been assassinated (not literally) many years before I took over responsibility. Other managers try hard to keep people in the business, maybe moving them to areas where they will not do too much damage, or just closing their eyes to the problem. As I have said, I am passionate and my normal approach is to be friendly and approachable but I have no space for people who quit and stay. I have learned to ensure that, when people go too far, I take them out of the business quickly, but always with support. They're usually not bad people, they're just not aligned to our vision. There's a rule of thumb I apply: there will be a second conversation, but there's usually not a third conversation.

It is vital to confront these situations. You try to do it with humility. You always do it with respect, whether the team member is a director or a trainee. You do it with the objective of improving the business. But you do it.

There is another category of people, who are not as immediately damaging, but in the long term equally destructive. Some people will not want to come on this journey. This is not for them. Find something better for them to do. It's out there. I have spent weeks, months and even years trying to convince some of the people I worked with. I know now: without their commitment, it won't work.

Compared to the number of people I have worked with, I have removed very few people from the business for this reason, and I am proud with what teams that I inherited have achieved when I was leader. The joke about being a smiling assassin didn't last long – but it has a serious side. It was clear that we were committed to achieve our shared vision of success, and if you didn't want to come on this journey, then you needed to find another journey that you did want to make.

Events

When he was British prime minister, Harold MacMillan was asked what he feared most:[2] "Events, dear boy, events," he is supposed to have replied. By "events", we simply mean the unexpected. We can't predict them, because then we would plan for them. Having carefully created your plan, you will be constantly tearing parts of it up and starting again. This will be difficult to do, but the apparent contradiction is that, if you want your 1,000-day plan to succeed, you have to change it. As I have mentioned, I review our plans every 200 days.

Sometimes the events will be so devastating, and go on for so long, that you feel you will lose faith in the process. If you lose faith, even for a few weeks, then the commitment that your team has made will collapse, and they would be right. The plan isn't a set of rules to follow blindly, but it is a discipline that isn't just for the good times.

At the end of Chapter 1 I explained that, when I had lost my passion to run BMW, I was attracted by a new adventure called CarsDirect, which had just landed $280 million of funding. This was a dot-com startup, and setting up its European business seemed like an exciting way to rediscover my ability to build something. When I left BMW, the October 2000 issue of BA *Business Life* magazine put me on the cover. "From corporate comfort to one man online," it said, "you're 41, head of one of the premium brands in the UK on a reported £400,000 salary, with two company cars and a chauffeur.[3] Where do you go next?"

I'd just started with CarsDirect at that time and, as the article records, the first day I walked into my new office, the culture shock was so great that I thought: "What on earth have I done?"

CarsDirect's US management who hired me gave us £25 million to build a business that would sell cars online to UK consumers. The dream was exciting, but the working environment wasn't. They put me in an incubator called Idealab which had created some of the hottest dot-com businesses at that time, including eToys and tickets.com. I was in a shared office with 30 other people working for startups, all of whom were younger than me, and all of whom knew how to get their laptops connected. I didn't even know what an incubator was. I couldn't focus, couldn't concentrate, so I moved out, rented an office and recruited a team with four or five people, and then we took on an analyst to build some spreadsheet models. The investors said: "Just get some revenue and then you're worth a billion dollars." And the more I looked at the spreadsheets, the more I realized that it wasn't going to work, because legislation in the UK was different, and the rest of the motor industry – not least BMW, my old employer – were afraid of how the internet would change their business, and so were also determined this wasn't going to work. Many companies were doing everything they could to stop us getting the cars we needed.

CarsDirect started to find itself in some difficulties in the US, and the dot-com crash had punctured everyone's confidence. There was a lot of activity, but I couldn't see any value creation. The US part of the operation wanted out of Europe, and wanted to take its money back.

So there we were. I'd given up "sitting pretty at the top of the corporate tree" (*Business Life* again) and I had three months' salary, three months' rent on our leased office, no customers, no business model and a laptop. But we had a dream, we had commitment and we had a process that I knew would work. We decided to create an online car leasing platform, and then white-label it to all big brands, and we would manage the platform and take a transaction fee out of it.

We couldn't find anyone to fund us, so we went to friends and family and we raised £500,000 and started a business called Epyx.

At this point, your mind is screaming GET OUT. Instead, I got further in. Because the dot-com bust and the recession had thrown a lot of online merchant businesses into trouble, they needed someone who could come along and help them fix it. I was as desperate as they were, and so I asked, and got paid £50,000 a month for helping them to survive and get their businesses back on track. That income allowed me to hire and invest in the business. I took on a long-term contract (which eventually became permanent) at EurotaxGlass's (see Chapter 8), which meant I had to move to Switzerland, away from my wife and young family. I was working 12 days out of 14, sometimes 18 hours a day, literally on my own. At the end of the day I would just go back to my flat, drink a glass of wine, eat a ready meal and go to bed. And then start again the following day. I was in Switzerland for eight years. But we kept building Epyx, and never lost sight of the dream.

We learned a lot about what we would do to keep a vision alive. I learned a hard lesson about personal cashflow. Most of all, we learned the value of trusting the process, and sustaining the dream by doing that – not for a meeting, or a few months, but for eight years.

We revised the plan constantly, executed it, made another plan, worked through that, and seven years later we were able to sell Epyx for just under £100 million. Then we able to sell EurotaxGlass's for €480 million too.

Impatience

Short-termism is on the rise, according to the McKinsey Global Institute.[4] It measured results from 615 large and mid-sized US companies between 2001 and 2015 and compared those businesses that focused on short-term value with those with a longer horizon. "From 2001–2014, the revenue of long-term firms cumulatively grew on average 47% more than the revenue of other firms, and with less volatility. Cumulatively, the earnings of long-term firms also grew 36% more on average over this period than those of other firms, and their economic profit grew by 81% more on average," it concluded. It quoted a 2016 survey by FCLT Global in which 87% of managers feel pressured to report strong financial performance inside two years, and 65% said the pressure on short-termism had increased.

You won't always be able to resist this pressure. I've done a lot of work with private equity firms who have used me as a leader to build value in the companies they acquire. They want to create value, exit by building and then selling the business, and they have a timetable. I know what I want too, and I also have a plan to create value. But this has rarely been a smooth ride, because I want to build great companies that will lead to big numbers, and they typically want me to quickly produce big numbers at almost any cost to the long-term health of the business.

I am a hard-nosed, driven businessman but I think that many people I have worked with in private equity see me – with my ideas about inspiration and vision and truth – as some sort of big softy. It is unfortunate, but it's part of the way they see their business, as a zero-sum game where someone has to lose if someone wins. I have always led the businesses to success. But in my opinion, private equity houses don't seem to understand that if they worked in a smarter way with their management teams, they would make more money. They intrinsically think it's a short, brutal competition, and so as soon as they are ahead, they want to blow the final whistle.

The problem is that by cashing in too soon, not only can you break the value that the plan was helping to create, but you can destabilize the entire business. I've seen it many times, tragically in at least one of the businesses for which I was unable to finish the project. It's even worse when the PE firm brings in a hard-ball player who's going to show us all how it really should be done, and the team that sacrificed so much is betrayed by its managers in the pursuit of a quick profit.

But the magic rarely happens quickly, and the transforming changes that can occur are structured in 1,000-day plans precisely because the vision is too profound for a month, or a year. Short-termism values "now plus 3%" thinking and loses sight of the transformational goals which it is possible to achieve with a consistent plan and an inspired team. I have written about how we break the plan into 50-day sections that contribute to the key projects and maintain momentum with visible signs of progress. It is key that for each of the 50-day sections you do not let short-term goals distract you from the vision. If you do, this will erode the team's commitment, create multiple versions of the truth, destroy creativity – and ultimately undermine you.

Hanging on too long

I'm often still here, at my desk, at ten o'clock at night. I do this because I love what I do. That means that I also know when the passion for a project dims and I have had enough, when I have been in one place too long and it is time to look for something else.

Remember that as an inspiring leader you are an agent of change. This means that, once that drive has slowed down, it's probably a signal. Some of the toughest assignments are the most exhilarating. In August 2013, in my first months at Fairline, when the going was tough and we were questioning ourselves, and our plans, I reminded myself of this by writing in my notebook:

Progress: make it

- *If in doubt, move!*
- *If you move, move forward*
- *Look to the vision*

And then I added:

- *If in doubt, move again.*

Moving again at that point was about keeping up the momentum at Fairline. But I also know the feeling of doubt inside, and you have to respond to it. At Porsche, I remember that after a few years I would drive towards the office in the morning, 10 minutes from my house, and I as caught sight of the office, I thought "I've just got time to get to the gym this morning."

I had been there 10 years, and most of them had been hard work. It was time to find another dream because if I was losing my passion, getting paid a lot and enjoying a nice car while contributing less each year, everyone else would have seen it, and all the plans, visions and commitment that I have spoken about and lived would have meant a little bit less each day. Sometimes, to sustain the improvement you have made, it is time to get out of the way of your team. They still want to fly, but they see the light in your eyes has gone out.

Learning to sustain yourself

Machiavelli, who arguably wrote the first book[5] on how to be an inspiring leader, asked: "Is it better to be loved than feared?. . . The answer is that it is desirable to be both, but because it is difficult to join them together, it is much safer for a prince to be feared than loved."

He lived in a time when boardroom arguments were settled with swords or poison (when he failed to meet his KPIs to the Medici family, his bosses responded by imprisoning and torturing him). It's not right to enjoy being feared but you will sometimes be forced to choose between being loved and being respected, and you will need to choose respect.

Don't like me. Respect me, but you don't have to like me. Respect will sustain you for far longer, because even if you are doing the right thing, the scale and ambition of what you do will upset some people, often your bosses who have tried, and failed, to do the same thing.

After a particularly tough battle with a private equity firm recently, I wrote in my notebook that a fellow director had warned me: "In a world where the hidden dagger is used frequently, expect to get stabbed occasionally." I added: "It shows you are a player, not an observer."

You will be the victim of some unfair decisions, be undermined by those around you and sometimes just have bad luck. You can sustain yourself by knowing the full value of what your team has achieved.

But you also have to know yourself. Just as I spoke about letting each member of your team play to their strengths, recognizing your flaws and getting support for them will sustain your leadership. It is strength, not weakness, to do this. For example, I'm not a good negotiator: I get too emotional. So I don't put myself in negotiation situations. So, Mark and Daniel, two CFOs who have worked with me for many years, would go in before me. They are both calm and objective, and I sit there and watch them as the conversation gets difficult, and think: *I'd have dragged him across the table and slapped him by now*. But they don't, and that's why we work well as a team. If you know your weaknesses, you can find help to counter them.

A lot of us read business books, admire the good ideas, maybe even make a list of them – and then do nothing. At this point, maybe you think *I'd like to do it, but I don't think I can commit to something like that. It seems so easy for other people.* I'd say: it is precisely because it is difficult that it's worth doing. Don't give up. A lot of people get frightened and walk away. Don't do that.

But this does not mean you shouldn't try to improve yourself. MBAs are often criticized, but I believe in the value of education. I did mine when I was very young, because I got a scholarship and it seemed like a good idea. I didn't know at the time that I was seeking wisdom. The technical tools you learn may be important, but they are not the key. The most important part of this is to learn to think, to analyse the situation or the process, not just respond.

Make it count

I promised at the beginning of this book that you can inspire yourself, and the people around you, to achieve extraordinary things together. But this chapter shows that improvements can be fragile, can be undermined by misguided people doing what they think is right. Also, you can undermine them yourself. If, however, you can create a situation in which you let go, and the vision persists, this is the greatest success you can have.

But, when you succeed, the benefits last a lifetime, and you can feel them in everything you do. In his book, *Above All* Else,[6] competitive skydiver Dan Brodsky-Chenfeld, who survived a plane crash that left him with a broken neck, broken skull, severe head trauma and a collapsed lung, explains how he went on to become one of the greatest competitive skydivers in the world, and carried that success through to all other areas of his life. "The pursuit of victory, of becoming a winner, always provides the opportunity to become a better person," he writes, "Don't miss out on it."

Kevin Gaskell and Matt Gaskell at the summit of Carstensz Pyramid

Adrian Hallmark, who worked with me at Porsche, and took over the business when I left, has since had fantastic success applying the principles we share in other businesses. Today he is Group Strategy Director at Jaguar Land Rover. He says:

> "Porsche was one of the most developmental experiences I've had in my career. Most of the time I didn't have a clue what I was doing, because nobody had done it before. We just had to get it done, and then we found out that, when we did it, we were better than most of the so-called experts. While you were doing that, you felt safe and trusted, and you trusted others to do their jobs.
>
> After I left Porsche, I joined Bentley. We took Bentley from 900 sales to 10,000 sales in five years, when the total global market was only supposed to be 3,500 cars. We completely transformed Bentley's markets using the same ideas and processes that we had used at Porsche. I believe that if I walked into any company that was demoralized, that if we made a plan and stuck to it, we could improve that business. Once you've done it once, you know that what seems impossible is possible."

Notes

1. Coyne, K. and Coyne, E. 2007. Surviving your new CEO, *Harvard Business Review* (May).
2. We don't know exactly which events he was referring to.
3. This is laying it on a bit. I didn't earn anything like that, and most of the time I rode my motorbike to work.
4. McKinsey Global Institute. 2017. *Measuring the Economic Impact of Short-termism.*
5. Machiavelli, N. 1516. *The Prince.*
6. Brodsky-Chenfeld, D. 2011. *Above All Else: A World Champion Skydiver's Story of Survival and What it Taught Him About Fear, Adversity, and Success.* New York: Skyhorse Publishing.

AFTERWORD: WAIT UNTIL THE SUN COMES UP

Being an inspiring leader is not complicated, but it is difficult, and sometimes you will lose sight of what you are doing.

I don't keep many things to remind me of the jobs I've finished. On my bookshelf, there's a replica of one quarter of the Porsche workshop that was given to me when I left, with little models of the cars I used to drive when I worked there. It's even got Cliffy, who I used to work with, sitting there eating his lunch. I've got a few pictures from my adventures, a model of a BMW engine that runs when the sun shines on it and a shiny cleat from a boat that I use as a paperweight.

But everywhere I go, I can carry two things with me that are worth far more. First, I know how meaningful success feels, the wonderful moments of knowing that the team has achieved what it set out to do. I also have freedom, the luxury of being able to choose to do (or not to do) the things that inspire me.

But, while you're in the middle of the struggle, facing problems and conflict and hours of hard work, it can be hard to keep a vision alive that what you are doing will lead you to success. The principle might sometimes be closer to another political quote, this one attributed to Winston Churchill: "If you're going through hell, keep going." I'd argue that if each day, month or year is better than the last, and you are following the process, that's success. Remember: this is the life you chose, and it is the only one you have, so don't be afraid to set out to achieve the vision of success you have for yourself and never let the dream go.

Some months ago, my son and I set off on an expedition to climb Carstensz Pyramid in Papua. This mountain is the highest point between the Himalayas and the Andes, and the highest island peak in the world. It is one of the seven summits and even getting to the mountain is a slog: we flew for three days, finally landing in a six-seater aircraft on a dirt strip cut into the edge of the Papuan jungle. As we left the plane, local tribesmen carrying blowpipes, bows and arrows and machetes met us. They wanted our money, clothes and equipment. After negotiating with them for hours (and even employing some as porters) we set off towards the mountain.

For seven days we trekked through deep jungle, crossed rivers, struggled over fallen trees, all the way fighting off mosquitoes and illness. Eventually we entered the foothills of the Sudirman mountain range. Two days later, we arrived exhausted at the valley below the sheer limestone face of Carstensz Pyramid. We rested for a day to acclimatize, then set off to attempt the summit. It meant starting at 2am to get ahead of the sun: it would beat down on us, make the snow fragile and risk an avalanche.

The climb is technical. The rock faces are very sharp and aggressive. In the dark, we could not see where we had been, or where we were going. It felt painfully slow. But as we tired, and our enthusiasm waned, our guide kept saying to us, *wait until the sun comes up – and then you will see.*

So we struggled on. Difficult, dangerous, tiring.

At 6am we watched the sun rise. For the first time, we saw how far we had climbed. We could see the summit. The world was immediately a better and more positive place. Our guide knew that daylight would give us the energy and determination to succeed.

Four hours later we stood on the highest point in Australasia. We had committed to reach the summit, connected the team with a plan and then created the magical experience of standing together with the whole of Australasia beneath our feet. At that moment, all the darkness, difficulty and discomfort was forgotten.

Our guide was an inspiring leader.

Now it's your turn to be an inspiring leader. To dream of reaching the top of your mountain. Shine a light on the summit and invite your team to share the climb. Plan your route. Recognize that there will be difficult parts and that sometimes it will rain. If you work as a team, share the load and climb from ridge to ridge you will make it. Make sure you have fun on the journey because the view from the top will be sensational.

Good luck in finding your adventure. Let me know how you get on.

BIBLIOGRAPHY

Abrashoff, M. 2002. *It's Your Ship: Management Techniques from the Best Damn Ship in the Navy*. New York: Business Plus Books.

Amabile, T. and Kramer, S. 2011. The power of small wins, *Harvard Business Review* (May).

Amabile, T. and Kramer, S. 2017. *The Progress Principle: Using Small Wins to Ignite Joy, Engagement, and Creativity at Work*. Boston: Harvard Business Review Press.

American Psychological Association. 2012. *What You Need to Know about Willpower: The Psychological Science of Self-control*.

Anthony, S. 2016. What do you really mean by business "transformation"? *Harvard Business Review*, 29 February.

Autobild. 2015. *Wiedeking verdiente über 100 Millionen*.

Barsh, J., Capozzi, M. and Davidson, J. 2008. Leadership and innovation, *McKinsey Quarterly* (January).

Bass, B. 1985. *Leadership and Performance Beyond Expectations*. New York: Collier Macmillan.

Brodsky-Chenfeld, D. 2011. *Above All Else: A World Champion Skydiver's Story of Survival and What It Taught Him About Fear, Adversity, and Success*. New York: Skyhorse Publishing.

Burrell, T. 2017. A meaning to life: how a sense of purpose can keep you healthy, *New Scientist*, 25 January.

CB Insights. 2017. *The Top 20 Reasons Startups Fail*. New York: CB Insights.

Chambers, A. and Hale, R. 2009. *Keep Walking: Leadership Learning in Action*. London: MX Publishing.

Christensen, C. and Overdorf, M. 2000. Meeting the challenge of disruptive change, *Harvard Business Review* (March–April).

Collins, J. and Porras, J. 1994. *Built to Last*. New York: HarperBusiness.

Coyne, K. and Coyne, E. 2007. Surviving your new CEO, *Harvard Business Review* (May).

Edmondson, A. 2011. Strategies for learning from failure, *Harvard Business Review* (July–August).

Finkelstein, S. 2016. *Superbosses*. New York: Portfolio Penguin.

Gladwell, M. 2005. *Blink*. New York: Little, Brown.

Goss, P. 1998. *Close to the Wind: An Extraordinary Story of Triumph Over Adversity*. London: Headline.

Happiness Research Institute and TNS Gallup. 2016. *Job Satisfaction Index*. Denmark: HRI.

Hartley-Brewer, J. 2000. Geniuses "made with hard work, not born", *The Guardian*, 14 April.

Hayek, F. 1945. The use of knowledge in society, *The American Economic Review*, 35(4): 519–530.

Howe, M. 2001. *Genius Explained*. Cambridge, UK: Cambridge University Press.

Ipsos. 2016. Edenred Ipsos Barometer. *edenred.com*.

Isaacson, W. 2011. *Steve Jobs*. New York: Simon & Schuster.

Jenkins, P. 2017. How paying chief executives less can help corporate performance, *Financial Times*, 13 February.

Kahneman, D. 2011. *Thinking, Fast and Slow*. New York: Farrar, Straus and Giroux.

Kahneman, D. and Klein, G. 2010. Strategic decisions: When can you trust your gut? *McKinsey Quarterly* (March).

Kochan, N. and Interbrand. 1996. *The World's Greatest Brands*. Basingstoke: Palgrave Macmillan UK.

Lawson, R. 2006. The science of cycology: failures to understand how everyday objects work, *Memory & Cognition*, 34(8): 1667–1675.

Lykken, D. 1998. The genetics of genius. In A. Steptoe, *Genius and the Mind: Studies of Creativity and Temperament: Studies of Creativity and Temperament in the Historical Record*. Oxford, UK: Oxford University Press.

Machiavelli, N. 1516. *The Prince*.

Manyika, J. 2012. *Manufacturing the Future*. London: McKinsey Global Institute.

McDowell, E. 1993. Ritz-Carlton's keys to good service, *New York Times*, 31 March.

McKinsey Global Institute. 2017. *Measuring the Economic Impact of Short-termism*.

Meyer, J. and Meyer, J. 2016. *Handbook of Employee Commitment*. Cheltenham: Edward Elgar Publishing.

Muller, J. 2014. How Mark Fields overcame doubters to earn the job as Ford's next CEO, *Forbes*, 1 May.

Mundy, L. 2017. Why is Silicon Valley so awful to women? *The Atlantic*, 1 April.

OECD. 2011. *Work and Life Balance*. Paris: OECD Publishing.

Porras, J. and Collins, J. 2005. *Built to Last: Successful Habits of Visionary Companies*. London: Random House Business Books.

Pychyl, T. 2009. Fear of failure, *Psychology Today*, 13 February.

Rami, U. and Gould, C. 2016. From a "culture of blame" to an encouraged "learning from failure culture", *Business Perspectives and Research*, 4(2): 161–168.

Reingold, J., and Underwood, R. 2012. Was "built to last" built to last? *Fast Company*, 88: 103–111.

Resnick, B. 2016. The myth of self-control. *Vox.com*.

Robison, J. 2011. Happiness is love – and $75,000, *Gallup Business Journal*, 17 November.

Statistic Brain Research Institute. 2017. New Year's Resolution Statistics.

Thaler, R. 1999. Mental accounting matters, *Journal of Behavioral Decision Making*, 12(3): 183–206.

Valimaki, C. 2017. Formula 1 racing. *Chemical-materials.elsevier.com*.

Zuckerberg, M. 2012. Letter to shareholders, *Financial Times,* 2 February.

INDEX

processes 77–8, 107
progress 104–5, 119–20, 189–90, 235
project management 120–1
purpose xvi–xvii, 16, 22–4, 38
 building trust 186
 dreams 13
 geniuses 134, 135
 happy employees 182, 184–5
Purves, Tom 17

quality xvi–xvii, 76, 143–55
 Fairline Boats 38, 44
 total quality management 27, 150

RAG (Red, Amber, Green) colour coding
 system 125, 214
Rami, Ursula 213
recession 7–8, 232
recruitment 141
redundancies 36, 215
rejection, fear of 68
respect 171, 194, 204, 229, 230, 236
responsibility 59, 60–1
reviews 170, 230
Ritz-Carlton 26–7, 28–9
Rolex 21
rules, breaking 13, 17, 75

sales targets 17–18, 26, 29, 144
SAP 87
scapegoating xii, xvii–xviii, 217
Schulze, Horst H. 27
Schumpeter, Joseph 71–2, 77, 80n3
Schwacke, Hanns 131
scientific management 198–9
Scott, Lindy 114–15, 208–9
second-hand car market 136–7
self-confidence 6
service 24–5, 26–9, 32n7, 111, 202

setbacks 61, 212
shared purpose see purpose
short-termism 87–90, 233–4
silos 77, 109
Siltanen, Rob 11
situational model 6
skills 130–1, 141, 166, 206–7
small businesses xiv, 38
small wins 120, 189–90
"smiling assassin" nickname 229
social support 218–20
 see also support
Soviet Union 167–8
sportspeople 42
startup businesses xiv, 104, 179, 231
strategy
 BMW 18
 Fairline Boats 126, 224
 key strategic areas 110–11, 112
 team involvement 169
 Traderoot 91
strengths, identifying 84, 91–2, 220,
 236
stress 23, 60, 64
success
 360-degree view of 109
 defining 95–6
 feeling of 241
 illusion of 20
 as impediment to change 16, 77–8
 planning a culture of 121–5
 preparing for xvi–xvii
 sustaining xvii–xviii, 223–39
 teamwork 51
 Traderoot 98
 vision of 160
 "winner's curse" 89
succession 227, 228
sunk cost fallacy 92